DECISION IN VIENNA

The Czechoslovak-Hungarian Border Dispute of 1938

by

EDWARD CHÁSZÁR

Published by
DANUBIAN PRESS, INC.
Astor, Florida, 32002 U.S.A.

To the MEMORY of my FATHER

REPRINT BY HUNYADI M M K
HAMILTON, ONTARIO
1991

Catholic Publishing Company, Inc.
1739 Mahoning Avenue, Youngstown, Ohio 44509

PREFACE

Thirty-three years after the end of World War II the "European problem" still remains unsettled. Its most conspicuous aspect at present is that of security. The fear of a direct confrontation between East and West in Europe has been haunting the world for three decades. So far the attempt at reducing East-West tensions through the Helsinki Agreements of 1975 has not met with any resounding success. The prolonged—one may say "dragging"— Mutual Balanced Forces Reduction talks in Vienna do not seem to hold out much promise either.

Security, moreover, is a many-faceted problem, not confined to East-West tensions. Below the surface there exist tensions within Eastern Europe itself. The chronic instability of political boundaries in Eastern Europe is part of the problem of political security in that geographic area. The frequent shifting of boundaries attests to the difficulty of reconciling considerations of ethnicity or national self-determination with interests of strategic, economic and historical nature. Occasionally submerged, the question of boundaries keeps resurfacing, only to threaten the stability of the area again and again. Solutions imposed by great powers seldom survive the shifts in the distribution of power.

The study which is presented here deals with the boundary question of Czechoslovakia and Hungary; more specifically, with the boundary dispute of 1938, resolved at the time through an arbitral award.

The literature on the "Vienna Award", which followed shortly after the 1938 Munich Agreement and in a political sense connected to it, is rather sparse. Most of the material pertaining to this somewhat unusual arbitration is scattered in documents, memoirs, books and articles which are historical or political, rather than legal in nature. Consequently, while it would be relatively easy to produce a purely historical account of the event, an examination from the viewpoint of international law has been a more difficult task. The legal approach, emphasized here, should explain why a number of sources, ideological and polemical in nature, have not been utilized at all, but merely mentioned. This has been the case, in particular, of works published in the East European countries after the communist take-over. These works pretend to reveal "new material" on the dismemberment of Czechoslovakia in 1938 and 1939. In reality, all they offer is a Marxist interpretation of the circumstances surrounding the event; that is, casting everything into a framework of class conflict, and emphasizing the tensions between the "Western bourgeois states" and the "great Union of Soviet Socialist Republics."

The drawing of acceptable political boundaries is, generally speaking, a thankless job. Discussing it is usually a controversial subject. Still, I hope that my approach does contribute to the increased understanding of the Czechoslovak-Hungarian border problem and thereby, also, to its eventual final solution.

A word regarding the Documents attached: I sought to reproduce them without any changes, except cutting the text where it was clearly unrelated to the subject, and adding diacritical marks where needed. The exchange of notes between Prague and Budapest has been retained in the French original; otherwise all documents are presented in English.

Finally, I would like to express my gratitude to my former professors Alfred J. Hotz, Felix Rackow, and Herbert P. Secher for reading, and commenting on, the original manuscript before it was submitted as a thesis at Western Reserve University, and to Case-Western Reserve University for permission to use the original text.

I owe special thanks to Dr. László Sirchich for his interest in my work, his valuable comments offered at various stages of my research and the drafting of the original manuscript, and his encouragement to expand my work related to the boundary dispute. Francis S. Wagner in the Library of Congress was kind enough to facilitate my research in various ways. The Hungarian Association (Cleveland) awarded its Gold Árpád Medal to me for the expanded manuscript.

If, despite the help I received, there are errors of fact or judgement in the text, I alone am responsible.

Edward Chászár

Indiana University of Pennsylvania
Summer, 1978

iv

TABLE OF CONTENTS

LIST OF DOCUMENTS

LIST OF MAPS

ix

CHAPTER I

THE VIENNA ARBITRATION IN RETROSPECT

Facts of the Case

The Vienna Arbitration of 1938 between Czechoslovakia and Hungary could be conceived as a chapter in a longstanding territorial dispute, the roots of which reach back to the Paris Peace Settlement of 1919.

The Treaty of Trianon reduced Hungary proper to less than one-third of her former territory and about two-fifths of her population. Large numbers of Magyars were attached to the newly created neighboring States without plebiscites for the territories in dispute.

Although accepting the Treaty of Trianon as the law of the country by signing and ratifying it, Hungary maintained from the beginning the position that she would seek to change the terms of the Treaty by all available peaceful means as it was not a negotiated treaty freely agreed upon, but a "diktat," and as such, it was unjust.

Peaceful revision of the treaty was advocated by Hungary without success.

The action of seeking revision was warranted by the words of the Covenant and by faith in the future function of the League of Nations. For we may say by comparison that while the chief architects of the Congress of Vienna in 1815 prepared a permanent settlement, the statesmen of 1919 had labored under the assumption that their settlements would be but the ground on which a new kind of international relations was to develop, namely one conducted within the framework of the League. The organization was thought to be capable of dealing with all questions affecting peace and correcting all mistakes that may have been committed by the peacemakers.

As it turned out later, the League proved to be merely an instrument of the victorious powers to preserve the *status quo.*

1

'This fact accounted for the failure of Hungary to achieve peaceful revision. Her initiatives in the League and her attempts at direct negotiations with the "Successor States" failed.

Consequently, Hungary began to orient her foreign policy toward the *anti-status-quo* Powers; first towards Italy who was openly sponsoring the Hungarian revisionist case, and after the *Anschluss* of Austria towards her new neighbor, Germany.

It was at this time, in 1938, that Hungary had definitely abandoned the idea of seeking a solution through the procedure envisaged by Article XIX of the Covenant and joined the policies of Germany and Poland by bringing pressure upon Czechoslovakia. The aim of each of the three States was similar: the attainment of a favorable settlement of their minorities' question with Czechoslovakia.

As a result of the shifting balance of power the Munich Agreement was signed on September 29, 1938, by the four European Powers, arranging for the cession of the Sudeten areas to Germany.

The Agreement also stipulated for the settlement of the Polish and Hungarian minority questions with Czechoslovakia by direct negotiations. It declared that "the problem of the Polish and Hungarian minorities in Czechoslovakia, if not settled within three months by agreement between the respective Governments, shall form the subject of another meeting of the Heads of the Governments of the four Powers here present."[1]

While Poland achieved her aim within days by presenting an ultimatum to Prague, Hungary entered into direct negotiations. These however failed ultimately because the Czechoslovak Government "regarded as quite unacceptable the Hungarian demand for plebiscites in the disputed districts on the basis of the 1910 census."[2]

Meanwhile the British Government expressed willingness to take part in' a Four Power arbitration and informed the Italian Minister for Foreign Affairs that "His Majesty's Government are, in principle, in favour of the return to Hungary of those districts in which the population is predominately Hungarian."[3]

At the well calculated wish of the Czechoslovak Government the matter was finally referred to Italo-German arbitration. Foreign Ministers Ciano and Ribbentrop arbitrated the dispute, the latter supporting the Slovak, the former the Hungarian case. The Award was based almost exclusively on ethnographic factors and restored to Hungary 12,103 square kilometres (approximately 4,630 square miles) of territory with slightly over one million population, eighty per cent Magyars.

These are, in brief, the facts of the Vienna Arbitration. Looking at the case forty years later, a number of problems arise.

Statement of the Problems

The main problem is to determine whether the Vienna Arbitration was an instance of peaceful change or, by the use of pressures and veiled threats of force as instruments of national policy, a subversion of the existing legal order.

It is a difficult task to differentiate between peaceful and non-peaceful change.

On the one hand there seems to be a line beyond which the use or threat of force, and violations of international law will render, even if war does not occur, a given transaction non-peaceful.

On the other hand it appears that peace is not broken by all violence but only violence which defeats justice, in other words, by crime.[4]

Based on the concept that peace is more than the absence of war, that it is the absence of *injustice,* Quincy Wright defines peaceful change in the following terms:

> Change in law or rights through procedures other than war which are in accord with the international obligations of the parties concerned, or which the law recognizes as competent in emergencies to override normal rights and obligations in the interest of a higher justice or of the welfare of the community of nations as a whole.[5]

The above definition of peaceful change, if accepted, suggests several questions, both procedural and substantive. Let us attempt to formulate these questions.

Procedural questions. — What were the legal obligations of the parties to the dispute, or of others responsible for and involved in the settlement?

Were any of these obligations violated?

If so, were these violations justified by emergency, namely by the necessity of a speedy settlement?

To put it in other words: did the parties to the dispute exhaust the procedures available for peaceful settlement? Did the circumstances justify recourse to extraordinary procedure? Finally, was such a procedure admissible under international law?

3

Substantive questions. — Did the arbitral decision conform to general principles of international law, or to rules expressly recognized by the parties?

Was the decision substantially just? (Test of higher justice.)

Ultimately the above questions amount to the basic one:

Could the Vienna Award be sustained by international law?

The answer to this basic question will depend, in turn, upon the importance attributed to procedure on the one hand, and to substance on the other.

With too much stress put on procedures to the neglect of substance—in a society of nations which thus far had proven to lack either an effective machinery or the needed psychological support for peaceful change—all talk about peaceful settlement would be illusory.

Yet, to disregard entirely certain procedures which are by experience considered as most likely to yield justice would render it impossible to speak of international law.

In the mutual relationship of law and politics the legal order of a given time may have to give way to some extent to political pressures, for after all law derives its ultimate authority from politics. Nevertheless, political processes and emerging new political orders cannot, without impunity, destroy entirely everything that was built before in the legal sphere. To do so would be to destroy their own support.

With these warnings in mind let us now turn to yet another problem concerning the Vienna Arbitration. This problem is the following:

Nearly forty years after its conception, and with the status of the Award clearly defined by the Paris Peace Settlement of 1947, *is there a basis to admit the case for a re-examination?*[6]

Avid critics of the case contend that the Vienna Award was invalid from the very beginning as it derived from the Munich Agreement, itself a violation of international law.[7]

The problem, then, can be considered in different ways. The first way is that of examining the nature of the Munich Agreement at the time of its conclusion.

Responsible statesmen accepted it as a peaceful settlement since threats were superseded by settlement. Czechoslovakia accepted it, although under protest that it was achieved "without her and against her." The settlement was sustained as valid until Hitler violated its terms by establishing a "protectorate" over Bohemia and Moravia, promoting at the same time an independent Slovakia.

4

From there on the attitude toward "Munich" became equivocal. Czechoslovak politicians and scholars in exile had begun to point out that they considered the settlement invalid under international law as of its conception. Their arguments are respectable, but far from convincing.

The view of some of the Western writers had been best expressed by Quincy Wright in his work cited. Therein he cautiously holds that the placing of the substance of the settlement ahead of the procedure by which it was achieved rendered the Munich Agreement subject to legal criticism.

The official U.S. view was expressed only after the Second World War. Discussing the preparations for the territorial settlements of the Paris Peace Conference of 1947, John C. Campbell summarized the American position as follows:

> There was no thought of extensive changes or of an entirely new settlement. After all, the war was being fought against those who had violated the legal boundaries and had presumed to redraw the map of Europe to suit their own purposes. As a matter of principle, in the American view, the territorial changes made by Hitler and his allies must be nullified. On the other hand, the pre-war frontiers were not regarded as sacred. Demands for their revision would be considered, as far as possible, on their merits.[8]

This position is in conformity with the customary legalistic-moralistic approach of the United States to international relations.

Naturally in a world where, in the words of Julius Stone, the "crucial importance of the validity of treaties imposed under duress is insufficiently observed," the several views exposed above should not be surprising. Neither should they be necessarily the correct ones.[9]

Indeed, the opposite view is held by those who consider cession, be it voluntary or forcible, one of the main legal claims to territory.

"Involuntary cessions," wrote Professor Hill during the Second World War, "are often provided in treaties of peace, or they come as a result of a threat to use force." Pointing out several examples, including the transfers of territory after the First World War, he states:

> After a threat to use force, the Sudetenland was ceded by Czechoslovakia to Germany in 1938. In spite of the forcible nature of these contractual arrangements, they are regarded in international law as valid.[10]

It was certainly remarkable, and from the Czechoslovak point of view lamentable, that while during the visit of Beneš to Russia in December 1943, both Stalin and Molotov had promised to support the Czechoslovak claims to the pre-Munich frontiers, the British were still reluctant to give any promise of that kind.[11]

From all the foregoing it should be rather clear that, even if its status is now beyond doubt, the legal nature of the Munich Agreement is still subject to controversy.

Recognizing that the validity of the Munich settlement in international law was at its inception, the least to say, undefined, it would be incorrect to draw conclusions about the Vienna Award on this basis. That basis must be sought elsewhere.

Indeed, it can be detected by following closely the argumentation of Taborsky, learned critic of "Munich" and of the Vienna Award.

After making his case against the Munich Agreement, Taborsky states:

> Now I submit that if we consider the Munich Agreement as being invalid from the beginning, the Vienna Arbitration also cannot naturally be valid, and binding upon, Czechoslovakia. The basis for the execution of the Vienna Arbitration was Point 3 of Annex 1 of the Munich Agreement cited above, and the German-Italian arbitration in respect to this was accepted only in consideration of this provision of the Munich Agreement, and in view of the promise of guarantee contained in the Annex. If, however, the basis of a given legal action is, or becomes, void, that action becomes *ipso facto* invalid, together with everything that is legally based upon it.[12]

It is a fundamental error to designate Point 3 of Annex 1 as the basis for the Vienna Arbitration.

The Basis for Re-examination

Taborsky's error leads to the second approach concerning the possibility to admit the Vienna Arbitration case to re-examination. According to this approach the basis of that arbitration was none other than the *mutual agreement of Czechoslovakia and Hungary to submit the dispute to arbitration.*

This agreement was arrived at after renewed negotiations. Point 3 of Annex 1 served merely as a basis to initiate them.

The right to negotiate, that is, to enter into the political act of negotiating, either directly or through diplomatic exchanges, is not impaired by the nature of any previous action, be it a legal or a political one. To claim that the negotiations, leading to the agreement to seek arbitration, were invalid because of the alleged invalidity of *their* basis would be too big a legal *tour de force* to be taken seriously.

6

Taborsky compounds his error when he asserts that the invalidity of the Award is "not in the least affected by the circumstance that the Vienna Arbitration appears at a first glance to be in form an independent pronouncement and that it was made in the absence of two of the signatories of Munich."[13]

Regarding the first point he holds that the arbitral decision was "a direct consequence of the Munich settlement" and that a formal distinction between them "could not in the least alter their material and substantial interdependence."[14]

As for the second question, namely the non-participation of France and Great Britain, Taborsky construes it as a "further evidence of the illegal procedure of Germany and Italy."[15]

Furthermore he argues:

> Czechoslovakia accepted the offer of German-Italian arbitration under irresistible pressure and in a state of extreme distress through observing the indifference of the Western Powers, and knowing that to insist upon the participation of France and Great Britain would only exacerbate her situation, which was in any case desperate.[16]

Of these arguments the "material and substantial interdependence" is an important one. Unfortunately there is no proof offered to support its validity.

A close scrutiny will reveal, to the contrary, that the Vienna Award was not only in appearance, but in fact an independent pronouncement.

Long before the Sudeten problem arose Hungary had begun to pursue the question of a frontier revision. Aside from the initiatives taken inside and outside the League, Hungary had made several attempts to negotiate for the amelioration of the political and cultural life of Magyar nationals in Czechoslovakia.

Viewed in this light the problem had a substance of its own.

The Munich Agreement and the Vienna Arbitration were two separate transactions. Their bases, as it was seen, were different. So was their nature.

The Munich Agreement was an instrumentality produced in conference by four European Great Powers to settle the German-Czechoslovak problem. The procedure had been a choice of the Four Powers. The rights of Czechoslovakia to participate in the determination of the case were impaired in order to preserve—what was thought to be—the greater interest of the community as a whole.

In contrast, the Vienna Award was the result of a procedure chosen, certainly not free of pressures, by the parties as one most likely to result in a mutually acceptable settlement.

It will be the purpose of this essay to examine, among others, the circumstances under which this procedure had been selected and put to use, as well as the character of the pressures exercised upon, or by, the parties.

The non-participation of France and Great Britain, and other arguments against the legality of the Vienna Award, such as the absence of Czechoslovak parliamentary consent, or the effects of Hungary's annexation of Carpatho-Ruthenia in 1939 on the Award, will be dealt with in due course.

Suffice to say in conclusion that the foregoing does provide an adequate basis for a re-examination of the Vienna Arbitration.

In order to evaluate the case on its own merits and to study the settlement of the Czechoslovak-Hungarian dispute in a more objective light let us consider its antecedent to be not the Munich Agreement, but the development of the dispute itself.

The Background: Europe Between the Wars

Before examining in detail the developments of the Hungarian-Czechoslovak dispute in the summer of 1938, leading to the Vienna Arbitration, it is pertinent to comment briefly upon the general European situation within which the relations of the two states were set.

The decade after the First World War was a period of false stability. The peace settlement was too political. Geographic and political questions took precedence over economic and social problems. The political League of Nations was not implemented with an economic League of Nations.

The fact that the 19th century economic progress was interrupted by the war, creating economic and social dislocations, was not sufficiently appreciated. Neither was the fact that a return to the normalcy of the pre-war situation—instead of keeping pace with the march of times—was a step backward.

It was mistakenly assumed that peace had been achieved once and for all. Because of this attitude conditions became frozen. No effective steps were taken to provide for peaceful change as stipulated by the Covenant. The maintenance of the *status quo* developed into a guiding policy.

To implement this policy France had built up a system of alliances. One of the pillars of this system was the Little Entente. It opposed the revisionist tendencies of Hungary.

The distrust of nations for each other during this decade was demonstrated by a search for security, resulting in the Locarno Treaties of 1925, the Kellog-Briand Pact of 1928, the Naval Conferences of 1922, 1927, and 1930. In Eastern Europe the Soviet Union likewise had signed a series of pacts with her neighbors.

Of the above mentioned milestones there are two that bear particular significance for our subject. The first is Locarno. When Germany, France, Belgium, Great Britain, and Italy had mutually guaranteed German-French and German-Belgian frontiers as fixed by the Treaty of Versailles—and pledged to settle disputes by pacific means—France wanted, in addition, to guarantee the existing conditions in East-Central Europe.

Germany was opposed to this proposal. Britain, upon the attitude of whom much depended, appeared somewhat uneasy about the French hegemony in Europe and withheld her support, apparently because of the belief that no vital British interests were at stake in East-Central Europe.

The second fact of significance was the Kellog-Briand Pact and the imprint it left upon international relations between the wars. The Pact called for the peaceful settlement of disputes. Furthermore, as it was widely held, it "outlawed war." At the time of its signature by sixty-two nations, and for a decade to come, the world believed in its value. Consequently, at the time of these happenings the events of 1938 were judged by many in the light of the moral pronouncements of this document.

Shifting of the Balance of Power

The mid-nineteen-thirties signaled a turning point in European and world history. The postwar era of reconstruction and recovery, dominated by the Paris Peace Settlement, was coming to an end. The immediate background of this period had been a world-wide economic depression that had made peoples all over the world susceptible to new ideas.

The new era was marked by great conflicts of ideology, by a realignment of historical forces, and consequently, by the increasing of international tensions.

The dominating event on the international scene was the emergence of Hitler's Germany as a great industrial and military power. Germany gradually overtook French leadership in Europe and imposed her will on the smaller countries in Central and South-Eastern Europe. At the same time Italy began to ascend as a Mediterranean Power.

Both in Germany and in Italy the new ideologies capitalized on the deep-rooted human emotion of patriotism and subsequently developed a militant, aggressive, and intolerant nationalism. National spirit intensified to an extent that appears in other nations only in times of wars or of grave crises. Indeed, Hitler and Mussolini conceived of the present as a time of such crisis.

By 1935 Hitler and Mussolini, quite separately from each other, had consolidated the power of their parties, coordinated political and economic activities within their countries, and their systems came to represent a thorough management and disciplining of the life of the nation, sorts of permanent mobilization to attain national goals.

Italy, at first suspicious of a rising Germany, established in Stresa a united front with France and Britain. The same year, 1934, also had seen the signing of the Rome Protocols between Italy, Austria, and Hungary. To prevent German expansion to the south and southeast, Mussolini supported Austrian independence, and Hungarian revisionist claims as well.

The moment came when both Germany and Italy—still quite separately from each other—decided to change the terms of co-existence. Had Britain and France been able to present a firm and united front, Hitler could have been stopped. Instead, the two had alienated Italy and helped indirectly in the creation of the Berlin-Rome Axis.

The Disintegration of the League Order

The continuing shift in the balance of power had resulted in a gradual disintegration of the order created by the League of Nations. Japan's attack on Manchuria and the establishment of Manchukuo had proved that the basic assumptions of the League order concerning collective security were false. The example served as a green light to Italy and Germany.

In 1935 Italy had attacked Ethiopia. As had been true in the Manchurian episode, this case again demonstrated that the League could neither prevent, nor stop, aggression.

In the same year Germany had acquired the Saar territory in a plebiscite, introduced universal military training and launched a great rearmament program.

The only action the League had taken was that of condemning the German action. At the same time, half-hearted sanctions against Italy were not sufficient to stop Mussolini, yet were sufficient to make him abandon the League altogether. Then, France and Britain being preoccupied with Ethiopia, Hitler had found the time opportune to militarize the Rhineland, using the Franco-Soviet Pact of mutual assistance of 1936 as a pretext.

Soon after, the Berlin-Rome Axis became a reality. It assisted Franco in the Civil War that had erupted in Spain in July 1936. Mussolini, concentrating his efforts on the Spanish affair, made it clear in April 1937 to Schuschnigg, Austrian Chancellor, that Italy would not give concrete assistance to maintain Austrian independence.

Thereafter, the National Socialist Party in Austria had been given a greater latitude. Within a year their leader, Seyss-Inquart, succeeded with Hitler's help in taking over Schuschnigg's post and from that position was able to invite Germany to "protect" Austria. In April 1938 a plebiscite had voted for union with Germany.

A few weeks later Hitler had threatened to march into Czechoslovakia in order to protect the German minority, numbering about three million and now asking for autonomy. Russia had encouraged Prague to resist. In May, Czechoslovakia mobilized. This was, indeed, a full-scale international crisis.

As a result of, and within the frame of this crisis, there had suddenly reappeared the controversy between Hungary and Czechoslovakia over the Magyar-inhabited parts of the latter, ceded in 1919. The final outcome of the controvesy depended primarily on whether France and Britain, especially the latter, would act to maintain the *status quo* in East-Central Europe, or would bow to the argument that the unrest of Europe was fundamentally caused by the injustices of the Peace of Paris.

These were, in short, the developments on the political scene of Europe. The evolution of the Czechoslovak-Hungarian dispute took place against this background.

The account that will follow here examines the Hungarian-Czechoslovak dispute, first from March 1938 to the end of September, that is to the Munich Agreement; second, in a more detailed way, the relations of the two States during the month of October, from negotiations through mediation up to the Arbitration in Vienna.

Notes to Chapter I

[1]Manley O. Hudson (ed.), *International Legislation. A Collection of the Texts of Multipartite International Instruments of General Interest* (Washington: Carnegie Endowment for International Peace, 1949), VIII, 134.

[2]E.L. Woodward and R. Butler (eds.), *Documents on British Foreign Policy 1919-1939.* 3rd Series (London: H.M. Stationery Office, 1950), III, 202. Hereafter cited as *British Documents.*

[3]*British Documents,* III, 202.

[4]To this we have to add "violence the justice or injustice of which is in doubt because of the comparative equality of the support given to each side," namely *war.* Quincy Wright, "The Munich Settlement in International Law," *American Journal of International Law,* XXXIII (Jan. 1939), 14.

[5]*Ibid.*

[6]Article 1, paragraph 4 of the Treaty of Peace concluded with Hungary on February 17, 1947, declared the decisions of the Vienna Award "null and void."

[7]See especially Eduard Benes, *Memoirs: From Munich to New War and Victory* (Boston: Houghton Mifflin, 1954), pp. 200-221, and Edward Taborsky, *The Czechoslovak Cause; An Account of the Problems of International Law in Relation to Czechoslovakia* (London: Witherby, 1944), pp. 1-21. Cf. also Hubert Ripka, *Munich: Before and After. A Fully Documented Czechoslovak Account of the Crises of September 1938 and March 1939* (London: Victor Gollancz Ltd., 1939).

[8]John C. Campbell, "The European Territorial Settlement," *Foreign Affairs,* XXVI (October 1947), 197.

[9]Julius Stone, *Legal Controls of International Conflicts* (Rinehart & Co.: New York, 1954), p. xxxii.

[10]Norman Hill, *Claims to Territory in International Law and Relations* (London: Oxford University Press, 1945), p. 159.

[11]Eduard Taborsky, "Benes and the Soviets," *Foreign Affairs*, XXVII (January 1949), 310.

[12]Taborsky, *The Czechoslovak Cause*, p. 22.

[13]Taborsky, *The Czechoslovak Cause*, p. 22.

[14]Taborsky, *The Czechoslovak Cause*, p. 23.

[15]*Ibid.* This view was shared by others. Wheeler-Bennett held the German-Italian arbitration "flagrant disregard" of the Munich terms. John W. Wheeler-Bennett, *Munich: Prologue to Tragedy* (New York: Duell, Sloan & Pearce, 1948), p. 297.

[16]Taborsky, *The Czechoslovak Cause*, p. 23.

CHAPTER II

THE ADVANCEMENT OF HUNGARIAN CLAIMS

Hungarian diplomacy was rather cautious in advancing claims to the Magyar-inhabited parts of Czechoslovakia. In fact, at first these claims amounted only to requests of equal treatment of the Hungarian minority. Gradually, however, as the crisis over the Sudeten territory developed, the Hungarian Government began to make overtures for a possible frontier revision.

The efforts of Hungarian diplomacy can be divided in two parts: the first dating from the Czechoslovak crisis of May to the end of the Runciman mission in September, the second from the September crisis to the Munich Agreement. Both periods will be dealt with here separately.

In addition, it is necessary to point out the similar efforts undertaken by the Polish Government. In the beginning they were quite separate from those of Hungary. Later they were co-ordinated with the efforts of Budapest. Therefore, it will be not uninteresting to compare the actions of the two Governments.

From May to September

After the *Anschluss* of Austria it became increasingly clear that the Czechoslovak Government would soon be obliged to make substantial concessions to the Sudeten minorities. As the likelihood of such a settlement emerged, both Hungary and Poland began to stir with a view to establishing claims for an equality of treatment of their nationals in Czechoslovakia.

In attempting to stake out their claims the two Governments had chosen different paths and were treated differently.

The Poles, expecting immediate German action against Czechoslovakia, had carried out partial mobilization on the Czech frontier in April, and, according to a diplomatic report "were apparently resolved in this case on themselves occupying the Teschen area so as not to have to accept it from German hands, encumbered with embarrassing conditions."[1]

14

After withdrawing their troops in May, they had received assurances from Prague that "the Czechoslovak Government would grant the Polish minority any concessions granted to the Sudeten."[2]

In July the Polish Government informed the French Foreign Minister, Bonnet, that Poland was taking her stand on the principle of equal treatment for the Polish minority in Czechoslovakia. A similar declaration was made to the British Government in July after the announcement of the Runciman Mission.

Finally, in September the Polish Foreign Minister, Beck, had initiated action on the diplomatic plane "to secure the fulfillment of the principle of equal treatment for the Polish minority which he had enunciated in May."[3]

This action included emphatic claims, announced in Berlin, London, and Paris, for a plebiscite if there was to be one in the Sudeten districts. Later, when the cession of Sudeten territory became part of the Anglo-French proposals to Beneš, Beck insisted on a new frontier delimitation between Poland and Czechoslovakia around the Teschen area.

These moves were accompanied "by more or less veiled threats that the Polish Government would proceed to direct action if their demands were not accepted."[4]

Hungary in Search of Support

In contrast to Poland's action in Paris and London, Hungary first sought to enlist the support of Italy and Germany. Both of them proved to be ready and willing to further Hungarian interests, provided the latter would pay the price.

Italy, secretly preparing to establish a protectorate over Albania the following year, urged the withdrawal of Hungary from the League of Nations. Germany desired Hungarian participation in "Operation Green," the military action against Czechoslovakia, still top secret, but already in an advanced stage of planning.

It took considerable skill on the part of Hungarian diplomacy to evade these demands without risk of losing the possible support for Hungarian claims regarding Czechoslovakia.

Prior to the steps taken in Rome and Berlin which will be taken up in detail later, the only event of some significance was the visit of the representatives of the Sudeten-German Party to Budapest.

Acting on behalf of the party leader, Konrad Henlein, they arrived in Budapest from Slovakia where the head of the Slovak

Peoples' Party, Father Hlinka, had agreed with them on the necessity for co-operation between the dissatisfied nationalities. Hlinka "bluntly advocated the idea of an independent Slovak nation, which must demand autonomy for itself within the Czechoslovak States."[5]

The Sudeten representatives in Budapest stressed the necessity for the Hungarian minority to build up their political and economic organizations. During these talks the Hungarian Foreign Minister, Kálmán Kánya, who had just returned from Poland a week before, made a remark in a very decisive way to the effect that "Budapest and Warsaw were of the same mind in regard to the political fate of Czechoslovakia."[6]

Whether Kánya was alluding to a desired or possible partition of the latter, is uncertain. At any rate, the anti-Czechoslovak attitude of the Hungarians was rather apparent.

Undetermined policy. — In spite of the revisionism openly represented by certain officials, Hungary at that time had no clearly defined policy, and the Government was quite hesitant as to what action, if any, to take.

As late as July 1st, to an inquiry of the Italian Ambassador concerning the Hungarian attitude in the German-Czechoslovak problem, the German State Secretary, Weizsäcker, explained that "of course the Hungarian revisionist aspirations toward Czechoslovakia were known." But what practical policy is to be adopted by Hungary if it came to a conflict, "did not seem . . . to have been decided yet in Budapest itself."[7]

The question naturally arises, why did the Hungarian Government, after advocating revision for twenty years, follow now this cautious approach to the problem of Czechoslovakia?

The explanation is to be sought partly in the change of the Czechoslovak attitude toward the minorities question, but mainly in the overall European politico-military situation.

Acting under pressure from Germany, and on advice from Paris and London, the Czechoslovak Government had decided in April to introduce a new nationalities statute to the Parliament. The provisions of the statute were to satisfy at least part of the demands of the nationalities, first of all, of the Sudeten Germans.

On May 18 the Czechoslovak press reported the conclusion of the discussions over the statute in the Cabinet and announced that the Prime Minister "will begin direct negotiations with the representatives of the German, Hungarian, and Polish minorities within the next few days."[8]

16

In addition, the Czechoslovak Government took another step, equally important for Hungary and Poland; namely, it decided "to accord to the Polish minorities in the Teschen area and to the Hungarian minority in Slovakia the same privileges that would be accorded to the Sudeten."[9]

While these actions of Prague certainly may have had a restraining influence upon Hungarian policy, more cogent reasons were provided for in the report of Mr. John F. Montgomery, American Minister to Hungary, dispatched from Budapest to the Secretary of State in Washington on June 2, 1938.

According to the information of Montgomery, obtained from the Foreign Minister and from the leader of the opposition in the Hungarian Parliament, Dr. Eckhardt, "it was the agreed policy that Hungary would remain completely neutral in the event of a war and would take no action towards Czechoslovakia that would disturb the peace of Europe."[10]

As Dr. Eckhardt explained to the American Minister, this policy was based upon the following three points:

> 1) Yugoslavia and Rumania are bound under the Little Entente agreement to aid Czechoslovakia in case of attack by Hungary, and Yugoslavia in particular is not averse to taking over some Hungarian territory should the occasion therefor arise;
>
> 2) Hungary cannot afford to go into war and desires to remain neutral. To act in conjunction with Germany would make her an ally of that country, which would be extremely dangerous, and if war resulted Hungary would be dragged in;
>
> 3) In case of the breaking up of Czechoslovakia, Slovakia would naturally return to Hungary. Poland desires a common frontier with Hungary and would use every influence to that end. If Hungary does not disturb the peace of Europe her chances of getting back some of its lost provinces are better than if she involved herself at the start.[11]

After strong and repeated assurances on the part of Hungarian statesmen of the absence of any agreement between the Hungarian and German Governments with regard to Czechoslovakia, or of some secret understanding of any kind, the American Minister concluded his report "convinced that the above represents the present policy of the Hungarian Government."

Finally, the Hungarian Government seemed to appraise the European situation in the light of French and British pronouncements concerning the German-Czechoslovak problem. These pronouncements had left little doubt that the two Governments did not write off East-Central Europe as being exclusively in the German sphere of interest, and considered any change there as the common concern of European Powers.

Correspondingly, the Hungarian diplomacy in its dealings with the West seems to have tried to present the neutral course, thrust upon her by political realities, as conscious choice, building thereby goodwill for the eventuality of a future settlement.[12]

True enough, the earlier British attitude was that of reserving the right to examine these East-Central European questions "within the framework of Geneva." Yet, it was also known to the Hungarians from the Grandi-Eden talks of December, 1937, that in the opinion of the British these questions "did not present any insurmountable difficulties."[13]

Indeed, the announcement of the Runciman Mission, at the end of July, had increased the hope of the Hungarian Government about the British recognition of the importance of the nationalities question in East-Central Europe and of its possible solution.

The British Foreign Minister, Viscount Halifax, while informing the Parliament that the idea of the Mission originated in the German-Czech dispute, spoke also of other nationalities such as the Polish and Hungarians. Furthermore, the Czechoslovak Government in accepting the Mission referred to "nationalities" in the plural. Subsequently both the Hungarian and Polish Governments took steps asking that Lord Runciman consider also the case of their nationals in Czechoslovakia. The answer, however, to both Governments was evasive.[14]

Hungarian statesmen visit Rome. — Meanwhile, in the middle of July the Hungarian Prime Minister, Béla Imrédy, and Foreign Minister Kánya set out to Rome to discuss the Czechoslovak crisis. The visit was primarily the result of Hungarian preoccupation with possible Yugoslav action in case of an open conflict with Czechoslovakia.

Earlier in May, Mussolini had laid down certain principles for Italian policy toward Budapest. "In the event of Hungarian action against Czechoslovakia with German connivance," recorded Ciano, "we remain disinterested; in the event of an unprovoked attack by Yugoslavia (an absurd supposition, which may be ruled out) we would help Hungary."[15]

In order to weaken the League of Nations, Hungary was expected to withdraw her membership in return forItalian support.[16]

The Hungarian statesmen now wanted to obtain a direct guarantee from Italy against Yugoslavia in the form of a military assistance pact. While reassuring them, in view of earlier Yugoslav-Italian talks, that Yugoslavia had no intention to attack Hungary as long as the latter did not take the initiative in a conflict with Prague, both Ciano and Mussolini refused military guarantee.[17]

As for the Hungarians, they made it clear, even before the Italians would expose the above view, that they had no intention to leave the League of Nations.[18]

State visit to Germany. — Throughout the summer of 1938 Germany and Hungary conducted diplomatic exchanges regarding the Czechoslovak question. These exchanges, apart from acknowledging the existence of the problem and mutually stressing the necessity of its settlement, did not produce any agreement. Because of this fact both Hungary and Germany attached great hopes to the well prepared and much publicized visit of Hungarian statesmen to Germany from 21 to 26 August. Regent Horthy and wife, Prime Minister Imrédy, Foreign Minister Kánya, Defense Minister Rácz and their staff made up the party.

Ironically enough the visit, instead of clarifying Hungarian-German relations, ultimately turned out to cause much strain.

First of all, the visit coincided with the publication of the provisional agreements reached between Hungary and the States of the Little Entente on August 23 at Bled, Yugoslavia. The agreements recognized on the one hand Hungary's right to rearmament and stipulated, on the other, the renunciation of the use of force between Hungary and the States of the Little Entente.[19]

Foreign Minister Kánya went to great pains to explain to Ribbentrop that the renunciation of the use of force became operative with each of the three States only after the still outstanding problems, namely those of the Hungarian minority, had been settled.

This interpretation was exactly opposite to that of the Czechoslovak Government, but the somewhat vague wording of the agreements had certainly permitted different interpretations. Ribbentrop, for example, had understood them as the renunciation of Hungarian revisionist aims.

At any rate, the West and the Little Entente had considered the conclusion of the Bled Agreements as a diplomatic victory against Germany, while the Germans were greatly annoyed and regarded it as a stab in the back.

Only after the Hungarian statesmen had decidedly declared that they intended to side with Germany in a Czech-German conflict, did the Germans begin to negotiate seriously. In a series of talks with the visitors Hitler and Ribbentrop pressed hard to commit the Hungarian Government to military action. Both had intimated that inactivity on Hungary's part might result in the nonfulfillment of her aims.

19

Thus, Ribbentrop had told Kánya that "he who does not assist departs with empty hands," while Hitler lectured Imrédy saying: "He who wanted to sit at table must at least help in the kitchen."[20]

Nevertheless, the repeated attempts of the Germans were unsuccessful.

Writing in retrospect fifteen years later the *Survey of International Affairs* summed up the situation as follows:

> During these negotiations the Hungarian Government had resisted all the pressure that was put upon them to give a firm promise of military co-operation with Germany in an attack on Czechoslovakia—a promise which Hitler was anxious to extract in order that "Operation Green" for the conquest of Czechoslovakia might be launched with the prospect of such rapid success that the Western Powers would be presented with a *fait accompli* and no general war need be feared.
>
> Not even Hitler's willingness, at this stage, to allow Hungary to acquire the whole of Slovakia and Ruthenia, could tempt the Hungarians, in their disarmed state, to commit themselves to military action against Czechoslovakia which might lay them open to immediate attack from Czechoslovakia's ally, Jugoslavia.[21]

To round out the picture one should also note that the affairs of Hungary at the time were still directed by men characterized by definite anti-German feelings.[22] These leaders of Hungary did not think that Germany could win if the conflict resulted in a general war and they were afraid of German expansion toward the southeast. Finally, they "believed that Western opinion could now at last be won over to accept Hungary's claim for a revision of the territorial settlement made after the First World War, if she confined herself to demands that had an ethnic justification."[23]

From the End of the Runciman Mission to Munich

On September 16, three weeks after the Hungarian state visit to Germany, the British mediator, Lord Runciman, departed from Prague with his mission unaccomplished. By the time he had persuaded President Beneš to meet most of the demands of the Sudeten Party, the so-called "Karlsbad Demands," the latter had advanced its position to a degree that the Prague Government was unwilling to accept. Nothing less than union with Germany was now the requirement of the Sudeten Party.

Hitler's belligerent speech delivered on September 12 in Nuremberg, and the failure of the Runciman Mission created a new crisis in Europe. War again seemed to be imminent.

The "third party" which had attempted anew to break the deadlock was again Britain. The role of the British can be best understood if one looks at the position of the other interested Powers.

The United States, as usual, had followed a policy of non-involvement. As early as March 14, 1938, Under Secretary of State Sumner Welles explained to the Czechoslovak Minister in Washington that with regard to the situation resulting from the *Anschluss* of Austria the U.S. Government "had taken no action, had made no representations and intended to make none." The policy of the Government, stated Welles, "was to remain completely aloof from any involvement in European affairs."[24]

Washington, of course, had watched the developments of the Czech-German conflict with great interest, hoping for peaceful solution and favoring the idea of a Four Power Conference.

Both President Roosevelt and Secretary Hull had taken some important steps in the last days of September to prevent war. Roosevelt had sent personal appeals to the heads of the Governments most concerned, while Secretary Hull engineered the sending of appeals to Hitler and to Beneš by a number of countries.

Yet, even there Hull had instructed the American envoys to make it clear that the soliciting of appeals on the part of the United States "does not in any way imply any opinion as to the point of the dispute at issue."[25] Czech, French, and British attempts to have Washington take a clear position had remained unsuccessful.

At the opposite pole to the American policy of non-involvement stood the Soviet Union, ally of France and of Czechoslovakia. Willing and eager to take part in European politics, she was kept out of the picture on purpose, because her readiness to send military aid to Czechoslovakia had produced vehement reactions in Warsaw and Bucarest. Although Rumania hesitated, the Poles were prepared to declare war if the Soviets were to send troops or airplanes to Czechoslovakia. To the dismay of the latter, France and Britain cold-shouldered the Soviet proposals in the entire Czech-German affair.

As for France, the Daladier Government had relinquished the initiative to the British quite early. Already on April 30, in a conversation with a member of the German Embassy, Daladier had stressed the importance of Britain, as a free agent exerting pressure on Prague.[26]

On May 16, U.S. Ambassador Bullitt reported from Paris to Washington the following:

Bonnet said that his whole policy at the present time was based on allowing the English full latitude to work out the dispute. He felt that if it were possible to adjust this dispute without war the British could do it and efforts by France could only muddy the waters since France was allied to Czechoslovakia.[27]

Now the British, who described Czechoslovakia to Bonnet as "a combination of rags and patches stitched together by the Versailles Treaty that no one should die to protect," had little intention of doing anything for Czechoslovakia except offering their good offices.[28]

Bonnet felt that this offer would turn out advantageously for France. If Prague should refuse British mediation the British then would make it clear that "they were not prepared to go to war in order to maintain the dominance of seven million Czechs over three and a half million Germans. It would then be possible for France to take a similar attitude." In case the Czechs should accept, there would be a possibility for peaceful settlement.[29]

If this possibility passed, there remained the question for France: What to do next?

During the summer of 1938, the number of persons there who believed that France should fight in order to maintain her traditional power and prestige in East-Central Europe had diminished steadily. Moreover, as Bullitt reported on September 15, "the conviction that the Treaty of Versailles is one of the stupidest documents ever penned by the hand of man is now general."[30]

Both Daladier and Bonnet fought the Treaty of Versailles in 1919. They were now convinced that the Treaty must be revised, and regarded the alteration of the Czechoslovak State as a necessary revision.

Referring to the deep and sincere belief of France in the principle of self-determination, Daladier stated the French position to the German Chargé d'Affaires:

If the Sudeten desired autonomy they should have autonomy. He was even prepared to say that if the Sudeten should desire to join Germany the French Government, respecting the principle of self-determination, would have no basic objection to this solution. What he could not permit was that Hitler should attempt to settle the matter by force.[31]

As it is known, the impasse of mid-September had been finally overcome by the visit of Neville Chamberlain, British Prime Minister, to Berchtesgaden where, indeed, it was asked that the principle of self-determination be recognized. This was approved by the British cabinet, then France concurred in the proposal that the Czechoslovak Government should be asked to relinquish the Sudeten region to Germany.

Chamberlain's second visit to Hitler, and finally the Munich Conference, had sealed the fate of Czechoslovakia.

The Munich Agreement created a new situation with regard to the Czechoslovak-Hungarian problem. The understanding reached at Munich had narrowed down the scope of the dispute, and it was now clear that the final outcome would depend on the parties themselves.

This was less than what the Hungarian Government had expected to achieve originally, yet, in view of certain events immediately preceding the Munich Conference, the Hungarians were glad to have received this much support at all. The diplomatic moves of the last two weeks of September had caused much concern in Budapest.

Germany and the Hungarian claims. — First of all the Hungarian Government had to cope with two additional attempts of the Germans directed toward galvanizing Hungary into action.

The first of these attempts was a strong rebuke administered by Göring to the Hungarian Ambassador, Sztójai, during their conversation on September 16. Reprimanding the latter for the inactivity of Hungary, Göring complained of the comparative silence of the Hungarian press, "complete calm" in the Hungarian minority areas in contrast to the Sudeten, and of the inactivity of the Hungarian Ministers in the various capitals, in contrast to their Czechoslovak colleagues.[32]

As a result of Göring's *démarche* the Hungarians promised more activity in pressing their claims—the press and the minority groups to implement this decision—and promised to demand a plebiscite. As a further result, the co-ordination between Budapest and Warsaw was increased.

The fulfillment of the first promise was put into effect immediately. As for the demand for a plebiscite in the Hungarian-inhabited areas, if there was one to be held in the Sudeten region, this question had been raised with London before.[33]

The second occasion that served to increase the concern of the Hungarians over their situation was the visit of Imrédy and Kánya upon the express wish of Hitler to his headquarters in Berchtesgaden.

Records of the meeting, arranged hastily for September 20, only two days before Hitler's second talks with Chamberlain, are incomplete. It appears that Hitler had once more offered the choice to Hungary between two alternatives, namely a "territorial," in other words military, and the "ethnic" solution.[34]

23

The reason for this seems to be the embarrassment of Hitler caused by Chamberlain's acceptance, in principle, of the idea of cession. If now the Hungarians provided a reason, Czechoslovakia still could be destroyed. Otherwise there would remain a Czech Rump State in existence, an "aircraft carrier" in the heart of Europe to be used eventually against Germany. If therefore Hungary was willing to act by making such claims and in such a manner which rendered an understanding with Chamberlain impossible, the problem could be solved. Otherwise the Czechoslovak problem was to be worked out along the "ethnic" principle. Here, however, said Hitler, Hungary could not count on German support.

Imrédy and Kánya somehow managed to talk themselves out of the painful situation. They used the old arguments of their August conversation with Hitler, and made vague promises for military preparations, namely the calling up of two classes, adding that these could not be completed within a couple of weeks.

Imrédy did promise, however, quite firmly, that Hungary would not guarantee the new frontiers of Czechoslovakia until her own demands were satisfied. He also promised to send Hitler a statement of Hungary's claims. The statement, putting down the cession of the Magyar-inhabited areas of Czechoslovakia, and the realization of the right of self-determination for the Slovaks and the Ruthenes as Hungary's demands, seems to have arrived too late for the Godesberg meeting.[35]

All this fell far short of what Hitler may have expected to achieve. Consequently, he did not include the immediate satisfaction of the non-German claims among his peace terms at Godesberg.[36]

Western responses regarding Hungary's Claims. — Nevertheless, if Hitler was unwilling to push the satisfaction of the non-German claims, it may well be pointed out that Chamberlain was not inclined to meet them either. "If Hitler insists on talking of these issues," reported U.S. Ambassador Kennedy from London on September 21, "Chamberlain will adjourn the meeting and return home."[37]

Soon enough the Hungarian Government, which by choice, or by necessity, had abandoned the idea of a "territorial" solution, discovered that even Hungary's ethnic claims lacked the support sufficient to make them prevail on the Western diplomatic front.

The reason for this seems to stem from the new policy initiated in London at the time of the first Hitler-Chamberlain talks and duly taken up in Prague. This policy aimed at detaching the

Polish and Hungarian issues from that of the Sudeten Germans, and to consider the latter alone as the one of real importance.

Hungary, which until now did not even have a feeling of urgency, began to suspect that the hopes she attached in Britain were misplaced. This suspicion had arisen first when the Hungarian Minister in London, recalled a few days ago from his summer vacation, received the answer to the Hungarian note of September 17, which had emphasized the Hungarian demands for equal treatment.[38]

The answer, given to Minister Barcza on September 20 in form of a *note verbale*, stressed the priority of the Sudeten question and included the following passage:

> His Majesty's Government fully appreciate the interest felt by the Hungarian Government in the future of the Hungarian minority in Czechoslovakia, but trust that they will be careful in the present delicate situation to do nothing to extend the scope of the present crisis, and will be content that their point of view had been placed on record and will receive consideration at the appropriate moment.[39]

Verbally Halifax said that, since in this matter many others were concerned besides the British Government, Budapest should consider the most appropriate method of raising it at a later time. He suggested that it was a question for the application of Article XIX of the Covenant.[40]

In view of the experience of two decades, the suggestion of Halifax must have sounded ridiculous to Barcza. He deposited a note which pointed out that since, according to unofficial information, the question of cession was to be raised at Godesberg with regard to the Sudeten areas, "the Hungarian Government feel that, on grounds of international morals and justice, the same treatment could not be refused to the Hungarian minority."[41]

Nevertheless, the view expressed in the British note continued to remain the official Foreign office view and served to discourage Hungarian reliance on Britain.

At any rate, the next day G. Knox, British Ambassador, could report the military measures taken by the Hungarian Government in view of the Czechoslovak mobilization.[42]

Knox also reported the following part of his conversation with the bitterly disappointed Kánya:

> The Sudeten territories, he said, had lain from time immemorial inside the frontiers of the Kingdom of Bohemia and the Sudeten Germans had in history known the Prussians more often as an enemy than a friend; moreover their case had been backed by threats and military measures. The Magyar minority, on the other hand had been an integral part of the Hungarian Kingdom, and their case had been put forward for many years with calm and moderation. Hungary had made it abundantly clear that she had

25

sought a solution only by peaceful and lawful means. Now, he continued, if I would allow him to speak with all frankness, it was sadly evident that it was not the moral wish to see justice done that lay behind the concessions we had wrung from Prague to the Sudeten Germans but the threat of overwhelming force.[43]

It is interesting to compare the situation of Poland with that of Hungary during the last week of September. Having taken up the policy initiated in London, Beneš launched an effort to alienate Poland from Hungary by trying to satisfy the former's claims separately. On two occasions, at least, the Polish Government received assurances from Prague for differential treatment. The Poles seemed to be willing to negotiate, but their demands exceeded the Czech offers considerably. Furthermore, they were backed up by the Polish military measures.[44]

Prague objected to this pressure. The British, too, warned Warsaw in a very vigorous note. The situation became tense and Poland's claims were still unsatisfied when the news of the Four Power Conference broke. Thereupon Foreign Minister Beck took the attitude that Poland's claims were not a matter for discussion by others, and sent an ultimatum to Prague requesting immediate cession of the Teschen area.[45] From here on Poland pursued a policy of her own without regard to the Munich Conference and achieved her aims in a short time.

The Hungarian Government, on the contrary, was quite anxious to get satisfaction through the Four Powers. The question was: How to achieve this most effectively?

True enough, Hitler did not press the Polish and Hungarian claims at Godesberg, yet he made it clear that Germany would refuse to guarantee the new frontiers of Czechoslovakia unless the guarantee was participated in by the two states. This helped the French and the British to realize the necessity of giving some satisfaction to the Hungarian and Polish claims as well.

Ambassador Bullitt was right in calling on September 15 the attention of Bonnet, French Foreign Minister, to the following:

By ignoring completely the Poles and Hungarians the British and French Governments were thrusting the Poles and Hungarians into Hitler's camp and were placing themselves in a foul position before the public opinion of the world. I pointed out that Hitler had taken full advantage of this gross diplomatic error and now was in a position to say to the Poles and Hungarians that it was he and he alone who would procure their minorities for them.[46]

The conversation must have had an effect on Bonnet, for the next day he expressed sympathy with the Hungarian position.[47]

There appeared additional factors working in favor of an "ethnic" revision for Hungary. These were the willingness of Rumania and Yugoslavia toward the end of the month, to see a restoration of the Magyar-inhabited parts of Czechoslovakia to Hungary. Yugoslavia even offered to mediate, provided that Hungary would give a satisfactory declaration concerning the security of Yugoslavia.[48]

For the British it took some time to take all this into account, but on September 29, while the Munich Conference was under way, Halifax finally informed Kennedy in London that "a settlement must be made also on the Polish and Hungarian question." To this Ambassador Kennedy added in his report: "For the latter I am sure he has more feeling in the righteousness of their case than for Poland or Germany."[49]

On the same evening, after new Hungarian urgings, Halifax sent a message to the British Delegation at Munich suggesting that "some cession of territory on the Hungarian frontier will in present circumstances prove necessary and that this fact should be at once recognized by the Czech Government."[50]

Nevertheless, this change in the attitude of Halifax came too late to have any effect at the Conference.

The Italians, aware of the fact that the Germans did not intend to make themselves the spokesmen of Hungary's claims, seized the opportunity to increase their prestige in East-Central Europe. Italy emerged from the Conference as the champion of the Hungarian cause.

Notes to Chapter II

[1]*Documents on German Foreign Policy 1918-1945. From the Archives of the German Foreign Ministry.* (Hereafter cited as *German Documents.*) Series D., 1937-1945 (Washington; U.S. Government Printing Office, 1949-1956), II, 451. Teschen was seized from Poland by Czechoslovakia in 1919.

[2]*British Documents,* I, 315.

[3]R.G.D. Laffan and others, *Survey of International Affairs 1938.* (London: Oxford University Press, 1951-1953), III, 50. Hereafter cited as *Survey.*

[4]*Ibid.,* p. 51.

[5]*German Documents,* II, 124.

[6]*Ibid.,* p. 136.

[7]*German Documents,* II, 448.

[8]U.S. Department of State, *Foreign Relations of the United States; Diplomatic Papers, 1938* (Washington: U.S. Government Printing Office, 1955), I, 506. Hereafter cited as *Foreign Relations U.S.*

[9]*Ibid.,* p. 522.

[10]*Foreign Relations U.S.,* I, 56.

[11]*Ibid.*

[12]This was particularly so with regard to Britain. There, unlike in France, existed some sympathy for the Hungarian cause, finding expression in the press, notably in Lord Rothermere's Daily Mail, as well as in the Parliament. See *The Hungarian Question in the British Parliament* (London: Grant Richards, 1933).

[13]*German Documents,* II, 74.

[14]Carlyle A. Macartney, *A History of Hungary 1929-1945.* Vol. I (New York: Frederick A. Praeger, 1957), p. 235.

[15]Galeazzo Ciano, *Hidden Diary 1937-1938*, trans. Andreas Mayor (New York: E.P. Dutton & Co., 1953), May 20, 1938. Hereafter cited as Ciano: *Diary*.

[16]*Ibid*. Cf. supra, p. 23.

[17]Ciano, *Diary*, July 17.

[18]*Ibid*.

[19]Monica Curtis (ed.), *Documents on International Affairs 1938* (London: Oxford University Press, 1943), I, 282.

[20]*German Documents*, II, 610.

[21]*Survey*, III, 69.

[22]In a way the next few months signaled a turning point. The pro-British Imrédy underwent a complete change of heart. Kánya, in turn, had to give way to the pro-German Count Csáky.

[23]*Survey*, III, 70.

[24]*Foreign Relations U.S.*, I, 486.

[25]*Ibid.*, p. 678.

[26]*German Documents*, II, 252.

[27]*Foreign Relations U.S.*, I, 501.

[28]*Foreign Relations U.S.*, I, 536.

[29]*Ibid*.

[30]*Ibid.*, p. 601.

[31]*Foreign Relations U.S.*, I, 581.

[32]*German Documents*, II, 816-817.

[33]*British Documents*, III, 1-4.

[34]*German Documents*, II, 863-864.

[35]Macartney, p. 267, n. 7.

[36]Afterwards Hitler bitterly described Hungary as one who thwarted his plans, forced him to accept the Munich settlement and thus gave Czechoslovakia a new lease on life. Had Hungary sided with Germany at the right time "he could have laughed in Chamberlain's face." See Hitler's interview with Count Csáky. *Documents Secrets du Ministére des Affaires Etrangères d'Allemagne,*

traduit du Russe par Madeleine et Michael Eristov (Paris: Editions Paul Dupont, 1946), Vol. II (Hongrie), pp. 74-76. Hereafter cited as *Documents Secrets*. As Macartney points out, however, equally important for Czechoslovakia was the attitude of the Slovaks, who, notwithstanding German efforts to stimulate them into separatism, had produced on September 19 a declaration in the favor of a "Czecho-Slovakia." In other words, the Slovaks were willing to go along with the Czechs if accorded full recognition of the Slovak people and language, and settlement of the Slovak question on the basis of the Pittsburgh Agreement. By this the Slovaks meant autonomy. Macartney, pp. 263-264.

[37]*Foreign Relations U.S.*, I, 631.

[38]*British Documents*, III, 5.

[39]*British Documents*, III, 11.

[40]Macartney, p. 260.

[41]*British Documents*, III, 10.

[42]By calling up two more classes in addition to three already serving, Hungary increased the strength of her Army, according to Knox, to 160,000. The Yugoslav estimate was 230,000. *British Documents*, III, 11-12.

[43]*Ibid.*, pp. 25-26.

[44]Macartney, p. 269.

[45]*German Documents*, IV, 6.

[46]*Foreign Relations U.S.*, I, 647.

[47]*Ibid.*, p. 710.

[48]*German Documents*, II, 936, 992.

[49]*Foreign Relations U.S.*, I, 700.

[50]*British Documents*, III, 48.

CHAPTER III

THE DISPUTE: FROM DIPLOMACY
TO DIRECT NEGOTIATIONS

In order to obtain on the spot support for Hungary, Count Csáky, Chef de Cabinet of the Foreign Ministry flew to Munich on the very day of the Conference. He carried a letter of accreditation from Regent Horthy addressed to Mussolini, and another letter from Prime Minister Imrédy listing Hungary's claims.

Csáky obtained an interview with Mussolini during the afternoon of September 29 and put forward the demands of Hungary: cession of the Magyar ethnic areas and plebiscites for the Slovaks and Ruthenes.

Mussolini, promising to present these demands as coming from himself, was interested most of all in areas claimed by Hungary unconditionally. He thought that their transfer might be put through immediately, with luck. Otherwise he would stipulate for settlement within thirty days. If even this minimum program was not acceptable, he confidentially suggested that military action might be the solution.[1]

As a result of his conversation with Csáky, Mussolini raised the question of the Hungarian inhabited areas but not that of the plebiscites, and submitted a draft for the solution of the Hungarian and Polish questions. It read:

> The heads of the Governments of the four Powers declare that the same principles which have permitted the solution of the problem of the Sudeten Germans should be adopted also for the analogous problems of the Polish and Hungarian minorities with a maximum delay of one month and according to a procedure which might be fixed through the usual diplomatic channels or by means of another meeting of the heads of the Governments of the four Powers here present.[2]

The British objected to the formula on the ground that it did not exclude the use of force, and themselves produced the following alternative:

> The heads of the four Powers declare that the problem of the Polish and Hungarian minorities in Czechoslovakia, if not settled within three months by agreement between the respective Governments, shall form the subject of another meeting of the heads of the Governments of the four Powers here present.[3]

This formula was adopted by the Conference, and attached to the agreement as a Declaration. In consequence, the entry into effect of the proposed international guarantee of the new boundaries of Czechoslovakia was postponed until "the question of the Polish and Hungarian minorities in Czechoslovakia has been settled."[4]

Exchange of Notes between Prague and Budapest

As a result of the Declaration, a series of diplomatic exchanges were started between Czechoslovakia and Hungary. These exchanges took place during the first week of October. Their purpose was to prepare the ground for direct negotiations. This was not an easy task, nor was it undertaken in an atmosphere free of disturbing influences.

Foremost among them was the difficult position of Czechoslovakia. The Prague Government found it quite difficult to handle the German, Polish, and the Hungarian questions simultaneously. In addition there were the negotiations with the unsatisfied Slovaks who now labored to change the structure of Czechoslovakia into a Federal State of Czechs and Slovaks. Meanwhile, the undefined attitude of Ruthenia added another element of uncertainty.

To all these came the reshuffling of the Sirový Government and the resignation of President Beneš.

The Hungarian Government, too, found itself in a rather precarious position. The pro-German "right radicals," whose number at the last elections increased considerably, regarded Munich as a failure of the Government of "moderates" to secure immediate satisfaction of the Hungarian claims. Large elements of the Army supported this view. The feeling was strong in Hungary that "Horthy and Imrédy have been too weak and unaggressive in the crisis of the past weeks, and that now . . . Hungary runs the risk of losing the Hungarian districts of Czechoslovakia."[5]

The outcome of the inner political struggle hinged now to a large extent on the success or failure of a speedy settlement with Prague.

On the external scene Hungary's veiled claims to Slovakia and Ruthenia rendered the situation very complicated. The future of these two territories was becoming an international problem.

Yugoslavia and Rumania, while reconciled to an ethnic revision, viewed with alarm the continued Polish-Hungarian efforts to establish a common frontier. Italy's Ciano favored the plan. The attitude of France and of Britain seemed to be equivocal. That of Germany was definitely cool.

Hungarian policy and its support. — While the countries mentioned were engaged in defining their position regarding the larger question of a possible Polish-Hungarian common border, the Czechoslovak and Hungarian Governments commenced the preliminaries to direct negotiations.

The Hungarian Government adopted a policy guided by four principles: (1) not to resort to force as long as the possibility of a peaceful settlement existed, (2) to insist in the determination of the new border on the same treatment that was accorded to the Germans and the Poles, (3) to settle the dispute as quickly as possible, and (4) to set up a new order based on self-determination.[6]

The Hungarian notes to Prague were geared to this policy. As Budapest was deeply suspicious of all delaying tactics, the urgency of the settlement was repeatedly stressed, and with the passage of time the tone of the notes gradually became less conciliatory. Measures of direct pressure were not introduced, however, at this stage.

In order to create a peaceful climate for the forthcoming direct negotiations, on October 3, Hungary invited the Czechoslovak Government to take certain steps immediately, namely:

(1) To set free at once the Hungarian political prisoners;

(2) To demobilize without delay the soldiers of Hungarian nationality, and to allow them to return home;

(3) To form detachments under mixed command for the protection of life and of goods, as well as for the maintenance of local order;

(4) To return to Hungary, as a sign of symbolic cession, two or three Czechoslovak towns adjacent to the border; the towns to be occupied by Hungarian troops.[7]

In the same note Hungary proposed that direct negotiations be commenced on October 6 in Komárom. In view of the governmental changes in Prague, the Hungarians later consented, somewhat reluctantly, to the postponement of the negotiations till October 9.

Hungary's repeated pleas for a speedy settlement enjoyed the support of London, Berlin, and Rome. To round out the picture, here are the main features of this support.

In London, the Hungarian Minister asked that Britain use her friendly influence in Prague to promote the success of the negotiations. As a result, Halifax asked Ambassador Newton to urge upon the Czechoslovak Minister for Foreign Affairs "the importance of initiating conversations with the Hungarian Government without delay and of bringing them to a conclusion as soon as possible."[8]

In Berlin, according to a circular dated October 1, "very far-reaching German diplomatic support has in principle been promised" to Hungary. The German view was that "incontestably Hungarian areas should pass to Hungary; even Germany has established no strategic frontiers but only ethnic frontiers." In addition, Hitler laid down the policy that "should Hungary mobilize, it is not our intention to hamper the Hungarians or even advise them to use moderation."[9] In the question of Pressburg Germany held reservations.

The directing of Italy's foreign policy was in the hands of Count Ciano, subject of course, to revision by Mussolini. Ciano, who for some time had been thinking about the feasibility of an Italian-Yugoslav-Hungarian bloc to oppose German penetration into Southeastern Europe, favored the idea of a Polish-Hungarian common frontier in Ruthenia. However, the question of Slovakia was something else; he was against the Hungarian plans. He told the Germans that "Italian policy regarding Slovakia did not contemplate handing over that region to Hungary." Rumania and Yugoslavia pronounced against it. "Italy did not wish to displease Yugoslavia in this matter."[10]

Behind the scenes the most ardent supporter of Hungary was Poland. After the satisfaction of her claims, Poland again took the initiative to co-ordinate her policies with those of Hungary. Although Kánya resented Beck's settling of the Teschen affair without keeping Hungary posted, on October 5 he sent Csáky to Warsaw to confer about the common line to be followed.

Beck at this time "was already prepared to let the Slovaks go their own way, but was strongly in favor of a *coup* in Ruthenia."[11]

The Hungarians, too, began to show inclination toward accepting the Slovak decision, whatever it might be, although they still considered the voluntary adhesion of Slovakia, including Ruthenia, "as the most practical solution of the Slovak question."[12]

As a result of the conversations, joint action for the re-incorporation of Ruthenia into Hungary was intensified. This was discernible both from the pronouncements of Polish diplomats in the Western capitals and from the activity of Hungarian irregular forces in Ruthenia. For, ironically enough, the Hungarian Government seems to have given secret consent to the use of the so-called "Ragged Guard," a rightist organization.

The volunteers of this irregular force, numbering approximately one thousand selected men, were encamped opposite the Czechoslovak border and made, in disguise, occasional incursions into Czechoslovak territory. Although their task was primarily that of propaganda, the operation certainly did not contribute to the "peaceful atmosphere" of the negotiations.[13]

Czechoslovak policy and its support. — On October 5, after the re-organization of the Government, Prime Minister Sirový described his country's foreign policy in a radio speech as simply one of friendly relations with all States, especially with its neighbors. He also referred to the country's other great problem, namely the coming transformation of the State into a Federation of Czechs, Slovaks, and Ruthenes.

The same evening President Beneš, in his farewell speech, compared the emerging "national state" with the former Czechoslovakia. He spoke of the "national state" as one with a "strong moral basis such as it did not previously possess."[14]

As regards the satisfaction of Hungarian claims, the outgoing Foreign Minister, Krofta, addressed on October 1, a note to the Hungarian Minister. Krofta stated that the "Czechoslovak Government were ready to open negotiations to arrive at an amicable agreement," and suggested the establishment of a commission of experts to discuss the whole question.[15] Two days later he made it clear verbally to the Hungarian Minister that the cession of Czechoslovak territory was a "definite and early intention" of his Government.[16]

The Hungarian Government, obviously pleased by the exit of Beneš, had watched with some anxiety the appointment of the new Foreign Minister, František Chvalkovský. Serving now in Rome, he was an experienced diplomat who had previously seen service in Tokyo, Washington, and Berlin. What is more, he was allegedly pro-Axis, or at least inclined to follow a pro-Axis policy. His appointment raised the fear in Budapest that Czechoslovakia would soon become a German customer, and as such would be shielded against the Hungarians by Germany herself. The fear was not without foundation.

Under these circumstances the Hungarian Government felt even more anxious to seek a speedy settlement. To its relief the necessity of this had already been urged upon Chvalkovský by Mussolini and Ciano, as well as the British and German Ambassadors, before his departure for Prague.

Chvalkovský described on these occasions as "imminent" the settlement of the Hungarian question, presuming that the Hungarian claims referred to the border areas. Yet, he considered the future of the Slovaks as "first and foremost a domestic affair."[17]

In this spirit the Czechoslovak Government renewed through British and German channels its assurances to the impatient Hungarians concerning the sincere desire of Czechoslovakia to reach an early agreement. At the same time both London and Berlin were asked to use their moderating influence at Budapest, for the Prague Government thought it imperative that the agreement involving transfer of territory "should not be done under pressure from Hungary."[18]

As a matter of fact, Prague considered the presence of Hungarian irregulars on Slovak soil as sufficient reason to refuse symbolic cession of two towns, demanded in the Hungarian note of October 3. Two more demands contained in the same note were evaded for various reasons, only the one concerning political prisoners was fulfilled.[19]

In the face of the insistent Hungarian notes to Prague, the British had complied with the Czechoslovak request for moderation. After expressing through Knox their "appreciation of the manner in which the Hungarians have hitherto put forward their claims," they conveyed the hope to the Hungarians that the latter "will in the future refrain from making demands in such a manner or of such nature as to prejudice the prospects of that peaceful settlement which the Czechoslovak Government have announced their anxiety to reach." As an added step, Knox was asked to communicate to Kánya the text of Sir T. Inskip's statement on the British guarantee.[20]

Whether the British had acted on confidential information or on a hunch, is unknown, but the forewarning was timely. In view of the repeated postponement of the opening of direct negotiations, and of Czechoslovak troop movements toward the Hungarian frontier, Budapest was at the time seriously considering military intervention to implement her demands.[21]

German support to Czechoslovakia came in another sphere, namely on the question of Slovakia. Although Germany favored the weakening of the Prague Government by advocating an autonomous Slovakia, she opposed Hungary's wider claims there. Speaking to the Italian Ambassador in Berlin, State Secretary Weizsäcker confided that the Germans "did not wish to hand over Slovakia to Hungary the more so as Hungary . . . had herself put forward only a demand for self-determination or autonomy for the Slovaks."[22]

Weizsäcker's interpretation of this demand was obviously not quite identical with that of Hungary.

Last but not least, Yugoslavia and Rumania had sided with Czechoslovakia on the Slovak and Ruthene questions.

Yugoslavia contented herself by registering in Berlin and in Rome her opposition to Hungary's designs on Slovakia. Her concern about Ruthenia was somewhat less.[23]

Rumania, on the other hand, took very active steps to offset Polish support of Hungary. Her Foreign Minister, Comnène, after intervening in the capitals of the four Powers, had brought about a joint representation of the Rumanian and French Ambassadors and of the Yugoslav Minister in Warsaw. In course of this representation, made on October 7, the Rumanian Ambassador was "especially energetic," and even hinted that "Rumania would have to reconsider her relations with Poland in the event of her continuing support of Hungarian claims in Ruthenia."[24]

The factors described in the foregoing were all working toward a limitation of Hungary's larger claims when finally the Czechoslovak Government informed Budapest of its readiness to commence direct negotiations. The delegation, said the Czechoslovak note of October 7, would have the authority to discuss, among others, the four points contained in the Hungarian note of October 3.

Negotiations in Komárom: Claims and Counterclaims

The delegates convened at Komárom (Komárno) on October 9, 1938. Hungary was represented by Foreign Minister Kálmán Kánya and by Count Paul Teleki, Minister of Education, an internationally known cartographer and scholar of ethnic problems. The two were assisted by a staff of experts, armed with statistics and maps.

The Czechoslovak delegation consisted almost entirely of Slovaks. The latter, having declared the autonomy of Slovakia three days before, insisted that the Slovak frontiers were their concern. The delegation was led by Msgr. 'Tiso himself, Prime Minister of Slovakia, and included Ferdinand Durčanský, Minister of Justice in the Slovak cabinet. The Prague Government was represented by Dr. Ivan Krno, Political Director of the Czechoslovak Ministry of Foreign Affairs, with the rank of Ambassador Extraordinary and Minister Plenipotentiary. Ruthenia, now also autonomous, was initially represented only by an observer, Dr. Zidovski, until subsequently, on October 11, Edmund Bačinský, Minister of the Interior of the Ruthenian Government, was appointed as official representative by Prague and joined in the negotiations.[25]

The Hungarians, as it was expected, decided to ask for the same terms that were given to Germany in Munich: ethnic frontiers on the basis of the census of 1910, and plebiscites in the other contested areas. Accordingly, they asked for the fulfillment of the demands contained in the note of the 3rd and for the unconditional cession of the ethnically Magyar areas. In addition, they had put forward the demand for plebiscites in the remainder of Slovakia and Ruthenia hoping that, if accepted, the Slovaks might, and the Ruthenes certainly would, vote for a return to Hungary.

On the first two points of the Hungarian note there was practically no discussion, since an amnesty for the political prisoners had been already issued, and soldiers of Hungarian nationality were being discharged from the Czechoslovak Army. Furthermore, the Slovak delegation agreed to hand over the railway station of Nové Mesto (Sátoraljaújhely) and the town of Sahý (Ipolyság) for token occupation.

At the same time the Slovaks insisted that the question of the future of Slovakia and Ruthenia fell outside the scope of the Munich Agreement. They were unwilling to discuss this matter.

There remained the ethnic claims of Hungary. The Slovaks did not argue the principle but were unable to agree on the figures presented by their opponents.

In the course of the protracted discussions the Hungarians presented the following case:

The Treaty of Trianon had granted to Czechoslovakia 62,937 square kilometres, or 22 per cent of Hungary's territory, and according to the census of 1910, 3,575,685 persons of whom 1,702,000, or 46.6 per cent, were Slovaks; 1,084,000, or 30 per cent, Hungarians; 436,000, or 12 per cent, Ruthenes; 266,000, or 7.5 per cent, Germans; 22,000 Rumanians, and 68,000 others.[26]

According to Hungarian statistics, the territory transferred to Czechoslovakia counted 13 towns and 830 villages where the Hungarians surpassed the 50 per cent proportion. The total territory of these towns and villages was 12,316 square kilometres. In 1910 they had a total population of 907,278, of whom 818,401, or 90.2 per cent were of Hungarian nationality; 61,373, or 5.7 per cent were of Slovak nationality, and 19,641, or 2.2 per cent were Germans.

The Hungarians transmitted to the Slovak delegation the map of the Magyar ethnic zone alongside the border, with the requested new frontier marked. The line proposed by Hungary included twelve out of the thirteen towns and 812 out of the 830 villages with Hungarian majority. Counter-balancing the villages of Hungarian majority that fell beyond the requested line, there were several villages of Slovak or mixed population on the Hungarian side, for one reason "because of their enclaved situation, for another, to trace the new borderline as reasonably as possible."[27]

The territory of which the retrocession was asked measured 14,153 square kilometres with a population counting 1,090,569 inhabitants of whom 848,969, or 77.9 per cent, were of Hungarian nationality, 147,294, or 13.5 per cent, were of Slovak nationality, and 63,927, or 5.9 per cent, were Germans.

Beyond doubt, there existed an ethnic line, by and large coinciding with the geographical line where the foothills of the mountains ended and the plain began. In the rural areas north of this line the population was Slovak, to the south, Hungarian. Nevertheless, the population of those towns that lay exactly on the ethnic line, in the mouths of the valleys, was very mixed and included people who were bilingual or of mixed origin. These could equally well be described as belonging to either nationality.

In addition, there were a large number of Jews whom both regimes counted on their own side for statistical purposes.

Thus, with regard to the string of towns of which Hungary had asked the restitution, the ethnic line was blurred. Accordingly, the towns were hotly contested.[28]

Slovak propositions. — The first proposition of the Slovak delegation consisted only of a promise of autonomy to the Hungarians of Slovakia within the Czechoslovak State. As Prague had already accepted the principle of cession of the ethnic areas, this offer seems to have originated exclusively with the Slovak Autonomous Government. The delegation pointed out in support of this offer that the Munich Agreement did not exclude such a solution. The offer was rejected at once by Kánya, who said that "he had come to negotiate, not to joke."[29]

After the Hungarian refusal to accept autonomy the Slovak delegation demanded a short interruption; subsequently it offered the "Velký Ostrov Žitný" or "Csallóköz," the island surrounded by the branches of the Danube between Bratislava and Komárom. The area of the island of Csallóköz, without counting the four villages near Bratislava, which did not figure in the offer, was 1,840 square kilometres with a population of 121,000, of whom 117,000 were Hungarians. This offer, too, was rejected by Hungary.

As the next step the Slovak delegation made a new offer on October 13, carrying, according to Hungarian figures, a total area of 5,405 square kilometres where the population in 1910 numbered 349,026 inhabitants, 341,987 of them Hungarians.

According to the terms of this offer 724,698 persons of Hungarian nationality would have remained in Czechoslovak territory. The second Slovak territorial offer represented only 38.3 per cent of the territory and 31.7 per cent of the population demanded by Hungary.

On their side and on the base of the statistics of 1930, the Slovaks maintained that according to the Hungarian demands, Slovakia would have to cede 11,268 square kilometres of her territory with 1,120,000 inhabitants, and Carpatho-Ruthenia 1,982 square kilometres with a population of 218,000 inhabitants. Thus, by surrendering to Hungary 670,000 Hungarians, Slovakia and Ruthenia would lose more than 650,000 inhabitants of Slavic race.

The second Slovak territorial offer was geared to the above estimates. According to the Slovak delegation the second territorial offer proposed to cede to Hungary 5,784 square kilometres with 395,000 inhabitants, among them 45,000 Slovaks. The 300,000 Hungarians still to remain in Slovakia would have balanced the Slovak minority living in Hungary, and estimated by the Slovak delegation to be 300,000.

The deadlock. — During the negotiations, the Hungarians had repeatedly pointed out that, contrary to the assertions of the Slovaks, ethnic conditions outside the actual border zone were irrelevant. In the Hungarian view, the Slovaks south of the main ethnic line, including a considerable number in central Hungary, were descendants of voluntary immigrants. They were citizens of Hungary who did not desire to join Czechoslovakia, and their Magyarization was spontaneous. At any rate, the Hungarian figure of those who declared themselves to be Slovaks according to mother tongue was only 104,819 in 1930.[30]

In addition, Teleki argued that the Czechoslovak proposals were based on economic, not ethnic considerations.[31] According to him the past twenty years proved that only the frontiers based on ethnic considerations are stable ones. Ways and means could always be found, Teleki said, to solve the problems of trade and traffic, if there was good will.

After the exchange of opinions the Hungarians asked for a recess to formulate their definitive position with regard the second Czechoslovak offer. When the meeting re-convened at 7 P.M., Foreign Minister Kánya announced that in view of the "unbridgeable abyss" which existed between the legitimate demands of the Hungarians and the Slovak counter-proposal, the Hungarian Government, on its part, "considers the negotiations terminated" and that "it will seek an urgent settlement of its territorial claims" by the four great powers, signatories of the Munich Protocol.[32]

Had the Hungarians waited a little longer, they might have come to an advantageous arrangement with the Ruthenes, for during the days of the conference events in Ruthenia took a turn favorable to Hungary. The two main political groupings, namely the slightly pro-Hungarian Ruthene Council and the Slavophile Ukrainian Council finally reached an agreement about the future of Ruthenia, proposing to demand a plebiscite for the whole area, rather than to have it partitioned by a cession.

Although the "Ukrainian" Edmund Bačinský was appointed by Prague to the job of representing Ruthenia in Komárom, the head of the newly formed autonomous coalition government, strongly pro-Hungarian András Bródy, insisted on his right to perform that task. Prepared to negotiate with Hungary independently of the Slovaks, Bródy flew to Komárom on October 13. He arrived "just in time to see the two delegations parting in anger."[33]

Notes to Chapter III

[1]Macartney, p. 273.

[2]*British Documents*, II, 635.

[3]*Ibid.*, p. 629.

[4]*Ibid.*

[5]*Foreign Relations U.S.*, I, 719.

[6]*Documents on International Affairs*, II, 353.

[7]Translated from the documentary collection of André Balasko (ed.), "II. Frontières Tchécoslovaques," *La Documentation Internationale Politique, Juridique et Economique*, VI (Mars-Avril 1939), pp. 25-26. Hereafter cited as *La Documentation*.

[8]*British Documents*, III, 114.

[9]*German Documents*, IV, 55-56. The question of Pressburg (Bratislava) was delicate. Now capital of Slovakia, this Danubian port had a mixed population of Slovaks, Germans, and Hungarians, neither of whom possessed a clear majority. Hungary claimed it on historic grounds. The reserved attitude of Germany had caused a new strain.

[10]*German Documents*, IV, 30.

[11]Macartney, p. 282.

[12]*German Documents*, IV, 32.

[13]Macartney, p. 279.

[14]*Documents on International Affairs*, III, 331-333.

[15]*British Documents*, III, 76.

[16]*Ibid.*, p. 81.

[17]*German Documents*, IV, 37-38.

[18]*Ibid.*, pp. 31, 36. Cf. also *British Documents*, III, 115.

[19]*German Documents*, IV, 36.

[20]*British Documents*, III, 116. In answer to a question in the Parliament on Oct. 4, Sir T. Inskip, Minister for Co-ordination of Defense, said that the formal treaty of guarantee had not yet been drawn up, but Britain had a "moral obligation to the Czechs." In the event of "an act of unprovoked aggression against Czechoslovakia" the British "would certainly feel bound to take all steps in their power to see that the integrity of Czechoslovakia is preserved." *Ibid.*, n. 3.

[21]*German Documents*, IV, 44-45.

[22]*Ibid.*, p. 30.

[23]*German Documents*, V, 311-312.

[24]*British Documents*, III, 138.

[25]For a complete list of the members of the respective delegations see the accounts of the Komárom negotiations in Magda Ádám, ed., *A müncheni egyezmény létrejötte és Magyarország külpolitikája 1936-1938* (Budapest: Akadémiai Kiadó, 1965), pp. 738-772. These detailed annotations reveal the unpreparedness of the Slovaks and their reluctance to meet the Hungarian demands. Their reluctance was understandable: The newly formed government sensed the political disadvantages of territorial cession as an initial act of its existence. Speaking of the Slovak delegation, Macartney said: "They had not been initiated into the history of the earlier negotiations, nor even supplied with the material prepared for the use of the Czechoslovak delegation, and their sole armour was a terrified and stubborn determination not to be over-reached." Macartney, p. 284. As for the assertion of Laffan *et al.*, that Ivan Párkányi, Ruthene Minister in the Prague Government, accompanied the delegation to represent Ruthenia (*Survey* III, 85.), there is no evidence of this in the minutes. In fact, the same source puts Párkányi on the same day in Užhorod, attending the meeting which led to the creation of a coalition government for Ruthenia. *Survey* III, 126.

[26]These and the following data were taken from *La Documentation*, pp. 26-28.

[27]*Ibid.*, p. 26.

[28]Macartney, p. 285.

[29]*Survey*, II, 85.

[30] Stephen D. Kertesz, *Diplomacy in a Whirlpool; Hungary between Nazi Germany and Soviet Russia* (South Bend: University of Notre Dame Press, 1953), p. 270.

[31] The Czechoslovaks afterwards told Newton, British Ambassador, that the proposals had been based "on ethnical results of the 1930 census tempered where necessary by strategic, economic and transit considerations." *British Documents*, III, 171.

[32] See Document No. 29a, below.

[33] Macartney, p. 287. According to Macartney's information, derived from conversations with Hungarian diplomats, both Kánya and Teleki were inclined to continue the negotiations. They believed that the Slovaks would offer still another proposal. (This assumption later proved to be correct. Newton was told by the Czechs that the second territorial offer "had not been submitted as their last word." *British Documents*, III, 171.) The decision to terminate the negotiations was produced in a meeting of Kánya and Teleki with Prime Minister Imrédy in Budapest between the morning and the evening sessions of the Komárom conference.

CHAPTER IV

THE SOLUTION:
FROM MEDIATION TO ARBITRATION

Explanations for the Failure of Direct Negotiations

Immediately after the failure of the negotiations of Komárom the Hungarian Government addressed identical notes to London, Berlin, Paris, Rome, and Warsaw. The note summarized briefly events pertaining to the Czechoslovak-Hungarian problems since the signature of the Munich Agreement, and described the main features of the Conference of Komárom.

According to the Hungarian Government the Czechoslovak offers amounted only to "frontier rectifications of certain importance." They excluded the retrocession of all the important towns of Hungarian majority in the disputed territory.[1]

From the maps and from the comments of the Slovaks, continued the note, the Hungarian Government arrived at the conviction that the Czechoslovak negotiators were less guided by the ethnic principle that formed the basis of the Munich arrangements than by strategic and economic considerations, as well as those of railway communications.

The bringing in of considerations not applied to the solution of the German and the Polish questions constituted, in the Hungarian view, a refusal by the Czechoslovak Government to apply the principle of equal treatment.

Just prior to the last session of the conference, the note explained, the Hungarians found their suspicion confirmed. The dilatory tactics of the Czechoslovak negotiators were geared to the regrouping of their armed forces. The military expert of the Slovak delegation himself had delivered a menacing speech over the Pressburg radio, followed by an appeal to the citizens and soldiers.

Instead of extorting thereby concessions from Hungary, as was evidently the Czechoslovak goal, the above manifestations resulted in the Hungarian delegation's determination "to interrupt these absolutely useless negotiations where the conciliatory spirit of the Munich arrangements has lost all grounds."[2]

45

In addition, concluded the note, "the provocative attitude" adopted by the Czechoslovak Government had obliged the Hungarian Government to take military measure, dictated "by the necessity of the situation and by the security interests of the country."[3]

The recipients of the note were asked to take the contents into consideration with a view to a speedy settlement, based on the right to equal treatment.

On their part the Czechoslovaks pointed out that, desiring to reach a "lasting, fair, and rapid settlement," they had agreed to open negotiations ten days after the Munich Conference, although the latter had contemplated a delay of three months. Furthermore, they had agreed to symbolic cession on the very first day of the negotiations.

Their proposal stipulated for the cession of 400,000 persons, including 330,000 Hungarians, and leaving approximately the same number of Hungarians in Czechoslovakia as Slovaks and Ruthenes in Hungary. Finally, "they had emphasized that even this proposal was not final and that they wished to continue discussions on basis of mutual concessions."[4]

The Czechoslovak spokesman accused the Hungarian delegation of submitting an extremely unfavorable, as well as unacceptable proposal; with refusing to put forward a second proposal despite the earnest request of the Czechoslovak delegation to do so; and of abruptly breaking off negotiations only a few days after their opening.

To the surprise of Ambassador Newton, to whom the above explanations were made, the Czechoslovaks "did not . . . challenge the main principle of the Hungarian argument that the 1910 census should be used as basis." They merely complained that "figures which the Hungarian delegation produced were entirely different from Czech figures based on the same 1910 census."[5]

Immediately following the rupture of negotiations the Hungarian Government sprang into quick action.

First, the Council of Ministers decided to call up five more military classes by individual orders. It was decided not to publicize this "partial" mobilization until the attitude of Berlin and Rome had been ascertained by Hungarian emissaries. Former Prime Minister Darányi and Count Csáky were slated for the latter missions, respectively.[6]

Second, to implement his parting words to the Slovak delegation, namely that he had "decided to ask for the earliest possible solution of the question from the four Munich Powers," Prime Minister Imrédy gave orders to the Foreign Ministry to apply to the Four Powers.[7]

The appeal was made in Paris by the Hungarian Minister in person. To London the request arrived indirectly from Rome, due to consultation between Italy and Hungary. Csáky flew to Rome not only to sound out Italian opinion on the partial mobilization, but also to ask for help in arranging a Four Power meeting.

Mussolini approved of the military measures. He was ready to make a public statement that the Hungarian action was "justi-fied."[8] At the same time Ciano launched preparations for a con-ference of the Foreign Ministers of the Four Powers. Through the Italian Embassies of London, Paris, and Berlin, he suggested an early meeting in Italy.[9]

Ciano also promised to assure Rumania and Yugoslavia that the Hungarian military steps were not against them.

German Mediation

While Csáky was in Rome, events took place in Germany in quick succession which cancelled out Ciano's plans for a conference.

Chvalkovský already had an audience with Hitler and declared his intention to follow a pro-Axis policy. Similarly, pro-German declarations were coming forth from Slovakia.

In order to offset the impact of these declarations, the Hun-garian emissary, Darányi, was instructed to express his Govern-ment's wishes to improve relations with Germany by way of making certain pro-German gestures in exchange for support over the present issues with Czechoslovakia.

Darányi's audience with Hitler had an unfavorable start. First he had to listen to Hitler's scolding of Hungary because of her previous attitude, and her lack of determination to achieve her rights by aggressive means. As for the Czech-Hungarian dis-pute, Hitler said:

> The situation was such that the Hungarians had previously informed him that the Slovaks and Ruthenians wanted union with Hungary at all costs. But today this did not seem to be the case at all. So from that point of view the result of a general plebiscite was extremely doubtful. The deci-sive factor in any case would not be who was right but who had the power.[10]

When Darányi informed him that Hungary was ready to mobilize, Hitler inquired whether she was ready to fight? If not, why go to the expense of mobilization? Anyway, Germany was

47

demobilizing and could not help Hungary. The latter must now adapt herself to what was possible. "The new Czech-Hungarian frontier must be based on the ethnic principle."[11]

The above statement of Hitler reflected his final decision taken a few days before.[12]

Besides stressing the necessity of an ethnic settlement, Hitler also indicated that he did not support Hungary's claims to Pressburg because the Germans never wanted to live as a minority under Hungary. The reference was to Hungary's controversial treatment of her minorities.

Hitler now spoke to Darányi in a similar sense. Ribbentrop was instructed to establish maximum Czech possibilities and minimum Hungarian demands. Since Darányi had no authorization to negotiate with Chvalkovský, whom Hitler had asked to stay in Munich for this eventuality, he telephoned to Budapest.[14]

The minimum demands of Hungary having been shortly established, Ribbentrop had a subsequent conversation with Chvalkovský and traced a line on the latter's map as one on the basis of which the Hungarians would resume negotiations.

As it turned out later, Ribbentrop, deliberately or just by carelessness, drew a line different from that suggested by Budapest. The Hungarians were ready for concessions in Pressburg and Nyitra (Nitra) in the West, but insisted on getting Kassa (Košice), Ungvár (Užhorod), and Munkács (Mukačevo) in the East. To Chvalkovský Kassa was indicated as disputable, the other two eastern towns as remaining within Czechoslovakia.[15]

This so-called "Ribbentrop Line," which meant one thing for Hungary and another for Czechoslovakia, should have served as basis for new negotiations.

Chvalkovský said that he would inform his Government of the German view. "He personally was in favor of satisfying the Hungarian demands to the fullest extent possible, especially as Czechoslovakia attached great importance to the guaranteeing of her frontiers by Germany." He thought, however, that it would be difficult to "induce the Slovaks to be accommodating, as Prague's influence over them was after all limited."[16]

Meanwhile Ribbentrop contacted Ciano and told him that Germany preferred to act behind the scenes. Acting on the favorable report of Darányi, and desiring not to annoy Hitler, Budapest now instructed Csáky in Rome to drop the plans for the Four Power Conference. Ciano revoked the invitations, but was "not at all pleased" over this course of events.[17]

A few days had passed when Ribbentrop, after ascertaining that the suggested line would be accepted as basis for continued negotiations, received a delegation of Slovak Ministers. The latter complained that the 1910 census which formed the basis of Hungary's demands, was "incorrect" and even "falsified." They asked the Reich Foreign Minister to help them in carrying through their proposals, "especially for reasons of communications and economics."[18]

During this conversation Prime Minister Tiso stressed the importance of Pressburg for Slovakia. He admitted that in case of a plebiscite on the 1910 basis for Košice, the Slovaks would lose the town.

Ribbentrop thought that the Hungarians should give up claims to Pressburg, Nitra, Košice, Mukačevo, and Užhorod. He instructed von Erdmannsdorff, German Minister at Budapest, to make representations to that effect. Finally, he suggested the resumption of negotiations through diplomatic channels.[19]

The Hungarians had already indicated their willingness to do so. On October 17 Sztójay had presented a memorandum to the German Foreign Ministry, suggesting the above procedural change. The Czechoslovaks were to submit a new proposal which then would either be accepted or rejected by Hungary. In the latter case Hungary was to ask for German-Italian mediation or arbitration.[20]

Ribbentrop dismissed the Slovaks by indicating that although the Hungarians did not definitely accept the line yet, there was a good possibility for further negotiations on this new basis. If now the Czechoslovak Government would make a new proposal accordingly, he would strongly urge Budapest to accept. Thereby his resources of mediation would be exhausted.

The Renewal of Negotiations

During the following days, when Hungary was awaiting with anxiety and impatience the new Czechoslovak proposal, activities in and around Ruthenia were intensified. Poland's Beck, who withdrew in the background on the news of the proposed Four Power Conference, came forth again with a plan to partition Ruthenia among Hungary, Poland, and Rumania. Because of the latter's objection, the plan did not go through. On the contrary, Rumania was ready to move her troops into Ruthenia if, in case of an uprising or outside aggression, the Czechs invited her to act.[21]

Hungary, on her part, stepped up the propaganda campaign in Ruthenia with the purpose of getting a declaration in favor of Hungary from the new Ruthenian Government. This event would have served as a cause for annexation by Hungary. In anticipation, Poland was moving troops towards the frontier for support.[22]

On October 22, amidst this tense situation, Prague forwarded a new proposal to Budapest, based on the "Ribbentrop Line" as the Czechoslovaks understood it.

This third territorial offer envisaged the cession of a territory of 11,300 square kilometres, registering, according to the 1910 census, 740,000 inhabitants; according to the 1930 census, 850,000 inhabitants.

The new proposals came rather close to the original demand of the Hungarians.[23]

Budapest expressed its satisfaction, but countered the note on October 24 with some amendments. According to these amendments the area now offered by Czechoslovakia was to be considered as undisputed, as well as to be occupied by Hungary immediately. The area still in dispute north of the suggested line, and engulfing the important towns, was to be divided into eight zones as plebiscite areas under international supervision. Pressburg was to be set aside for special conversations, and the Ruthenes were to decide on their own future.[24]

If Czechoslovakia did not accept these counter-proposals, the question of the disputed areas in the West of Slovakia was to be submitted to Italo-German arbitration; for the eastern areas Hungary proposed joint arbitration by Germany, Italy, and Poland.[25]

Before Prague replied, a few things had occurred, frustrating definitely the Hungarian-Polish plans for common frontier in Ruthenia.

Polish and French reports, stressing the anti-German implications of the Hungarian-Polish plans, had come to the attention of Mussolini. While at first he satisfied himself by terming the attempt at the encirclement of Germany as "absolutely ridiculous," he now instructed Ciano to take up the position expressly against the common frontier.[26]

The Poles themselves passed up the last remaining possibility. Germany, reconsidering her earlier position, appeared now willing to see a common frontier if Poland compensated for it by giving up the Danzig corridor to East Prussia. Poland refused this German proposal.[27]

Finally, the Czechoslovak Government, reassured a few days before by Rumania, sprang into action. On October 20 the Ruthenes produced another resolution insisting on the indivisibility of Ruthenia and demanding a plebiscite. This amounted almost to a declaration in favor of Hungary.

In order to forestall the latter, on October 25 the Prime Minister, Sirový, summoned the four Ruthenian Ministers to Prague to learn their attitude. Bródy answered in terms of the above mentioned resolution. Thereupon he was immediately put under arrest. The "Ukrainian" Secretary of State, Vološin, was appointed by telephone as head of the Ruthenian Government. He was willing to accept an ethnic frontier and rejected the idea of a plebiscite.[28]

Next day, Prague informed London that the Hungarian demand for plebiscites in the disputed areas on the basis of the 1910 census was unacceptable. Prague favored Axis arbitration and "wished to have the views of His Majesty's Government on their attitude."[29]

In reply, the Czechoslovak Government was informed that "His Majesty's Government saw no objection to the settlement of the Czech-Hungarian question by means of arbitration by Germany and Italy, if the Czechoslovak and Hungarian Governments agreed to settle their differences this way." It was added that "if the two parties to the dispute preferred to refer the matter to the four Munich Powers, His Majesty's Government would be ready to join in any discussion."[30]

Similar information was forwarded to the British Embassy at Rome for the benefit of Signor Mussolini.[31]

Request for Arbitration

Prague was now ready to answer the Hungarian counter-proposals. The Czechoslovak note of October 26 passed entirely in silence over the proposed Hungarian occupation of the "undisputed" territories. There was no reference to the proposed plebiscites. The note emphatically asserted that the problem related to the Hungarian minority only and added that, since the Hungarian Government did not accept the Czechoslovak proposals as they were, "the Czechoslovak Government agreed to submit the question of the Hungarian minority to an arbitral decision by Germany and Italy, signatories of the Munich Agreement."[32]

Finally, the note stated that in case the two Powers accepted Hungary's proposal to include Poland, Czechoslovakia wished to include Rumania as an arbiter.

Surprised about the proposal to submit the entire question to arbitration, the Hungarian Government replied on October 27. The reply attempted once more to extend the application of the right of self-determination by way of a plebiscite to all minorities requesting it. On the question of German-Italian arbitration the note stressed that its acceptance "implies the obligation to submit in advance to the decision of the said Powers." The note then continued:

> It is understood that the competence of the arbiters extends only to the territories in dispute and not to those on which agreement already exists between the two Governments and the occupation of which by the Hungarian troops was already asked in the note of 24th current.[33]

Chvalkovský answered on October 28 in a polite note. The question was that of the Hungarian minority only. He noted with satisfaction that Hungary agreed to resort to arbitration by Germany and Italy with the obligation to submit in advance to the decision. Czechoslovakia placed full confidence in this procedure which had been suggested, according to Chvalkovský, by the Hungarian Government itself.[34]

Chvalkovský could not share the view of the Hungarian Government that an agreement existed already on certain territories and proposed that the arbitrators pronounce also on this difference of views. He was sure that the question of occupation, referred to by the Hungarian note of October 27, would be regulated by the arbitral decision.

Finally, as a practical step Chvalkovský suggested that the two Governments make a request within twenty-four hours to Germany and Italy to undertake the arbitration.

Thereupon Hungary, until now saying only that she was prepared to do so, lodged her formal request in Berlin and in Rome for arbitration. Czechoslovakia did the same.

Rendering the Award

While Czechoslovakia and Hungary were exchanging notes, the would-be arbitrators, Ribbentrop and Ciano, were exchanging their views.

Interestingly enough, Ribbentrop at first was against the idea of a possible Axis arbitration. On October 22 he spoke to Ciano about the matter and "ventilated the possibility of a Conference of Four, though it was he who refused to consider it a week ago."[35]

In Ribbentrop's view arbitration was dangerous because it would end by satisfying neither Hungary nor Czechoslovakia, and by obliging the arbitrators "to have recourse to force in order to put our decisions into effect." Ciano enlightened the Reich Foreign Minister that "arbitration implies the previous consent of the parties to accept its results."[36]

Next day Ribbentrop called Ciano again. During these two telephone conversations Ribbentrop revealed himself to be quite hostile to the Hungarians. Ciano recorded:

> The truth is that he intends to protect Czechoslovakia as far as he can and sacrifice the ambitions, even the legitimate ambitions, of Hungary.[37]

One day later:

> He does not want the arbitration, which would oblige him to show himself in his true colors to the Hungarians. He asked me if he may come to Rome at the end of the week to confer with the Duce and with me in person. I replied that he may. What is he up to?[38]

Shortly after his arrival at Rome on October 27, Ribbentrop disclosed the real reason of his trip. Planning already for a world war, he came to propose a triple military alliance.

The Italians took a realistic attitude. The alliance, they said, already existed in practice in the form of the Anti-Comintern Pact. "Why open the door to rumor by a pact the only consequence of which would be to draw upon us the odium of aggression?"[39] Ribbentrop, expecting perhaps an acceptance of the plan, was taken aback when the offer was rejected by Mussolini.

In discussing the Czech-Hungarian question, Ciano had repeatedly pointed out to Ribbentrop the significance of an Axis arbitration; a "gigantic event" that would set the seal upon the fact that "all Franco-British influence has collapsed forever in the Danubian and Balkan Europe."[40]

Once Ribbentrop seemed convinced, Ciano set himself to the task of securing as much as he could for the Hungarians. Over the arguments of Ribbentrop, who "defended the Czech cause sword in hand," Ciano strongly urged that Hungary be given the three contested eastern towns. In return, Hungary was to give up her pretensions toward Ruthenia.

It may well have been that at this point Ribbentrop decided to oblige Ciano with a view to a future re-opening of the military pact question, a possibility not excluded during the conversations with Mussolini. At any rate, by the end of the day he had agreed upon the "advisability" of giving Kassa, Ungvár, and Munkács to the Hungarians.[41]

To Ciano remained the task of informing the Hungarians that they would have to renounce Ruthenia as well as the idea of bringing in Poland as third arbiter.

After these mutual concessions, there were indeed few differences left when the arbitrators met in Vienna on November 2.

It appeared that Ribbentrop had not definitely decided yet about the three eastern towns. He thought that if Hungary received all three, Ruthenia would be deprived of her economic centers and could not survive. In a final conversation with Ciano, however, he gave in.[42]

Decision in the Belvedere. — The arbitral session opened in the Belvedere Palace on the same day at noon. After the opening remarks by Ribbentrop and Ciano, the Hungarians and Czechs pleaded their cause. Kánya was "bitter and argumentative," Teleki was "calm and with more documentation." Chvalkovský was brief and left the task of presenting the Czechoslovak case to Minister Krno. In the view of Ciano, the Czechoslovaks "defended their cause well."[43]

Ribbentrop at this point showed himself much less an advocate of the Slovaks than he had before. In fact, he prevented Tiso, the Slovak Prime Minister, and Vološin, Ruthenian Prime Minister, from stating their views officially. "The views of both Governments," Ribbentrop said, "had been expressed by their Foreign Ministers." He could not see the point in listening to the statements "of a number of additional experts on the subject . . ." The two gentlemen, he added, "would have an opportunity for unofficial talks with the two arbiters in the course of the lunch."[44]

This was, of course, a procedure substantially favorable to the Hungarians.

The arguments presented in the course of the pleadings were not different from the ones already propounded during the previous negotiations. Hungary did not raise the question of Pressburg, nor that of the two easternmost towns, Ungvár and Munkács. The question of Nitra and Kassa was debated at some length. The discussions seemed to prove in general the difficulty of settlement along ethnic lines, especially where historical considerations were also at play.[45]

The two arbiters continued their conversations with the delegates during lunch, then retired with a small staff to prepare the Award. Ciano took control of the discussions and, except for a few disputed points, was able to trace the new frontier. Ribbentrop's unpreparedness enabled Ciano "to assign to Hungary pieces of territory which might easily have given rise to much controversial discussion."[46]

The day was closed by the reading and afterwards the signing of the arbitral award and the accompanying protocol. By virtue of the terms thus rendered, Czechoslovakia retained in the western section of Slovakia the towns of Bratislava and Nitra. Hungary recovered the three disputed eastern towns, in addition to four others in the central section.[47]

The area awarded to Hungary comprised 12,103 square kilometres (approximately 4,600 square miles) with a population of 1,030,000 inhabitants. The population breakdown differs according to the relevant censuses.

Knox, who thought that both censuses had a political basis, gave the Foreign Office figures which were believed to be approximately accurate.

The figures of Knox were:[48]

Hungarians	830,000
Slovaks	140,000
Germans	20,000
Ruthenes, Poles, Rumanians and others	40,000

Total: 1,030,000

Thus, the number of Hungarians in Czechoslovakia diminished to 66,000. At the same time the ratio of Hungary's non-Magyar population had increased from 7.2 per cent to approximately 9 per cent.

Conforming to plans worked out by a Czechoslovak-Hungarian commission of military experts, the ceded area was occupied by Hungary between the 5th and 10th of November as stipulated by the Award. On the latter date, the line of demarcation was fixed by the military commission.

The recovered "Highland Territories" were incorporated into Hungary on November 12 by act of Parliament.[49]

As a last step in the execution of the Award an agreement regarding the question of nationality and option was concluded by the Czechoslovak and Hungarian Governments on February 18, 1939.[50]

Notes to Chapter IV

[1] *La Documentation,* p. 2ᴑ.

[2] *La Documentation,* p. 29.

[3] *Ibid.*

[4] *British Documents,* III, 184.

[5] *Ibid.,* p. 185.

[6] *German Documents,* IV, 67-68.

[7] Macartney, p. 287.

[8] *German Documents,* IV, 69.

[9] *British Documents,* III, 174.

[10] *German Documents,* IV, 74.

[11] *Ibid.*

[12] The decision originated from the Supreme Command of the *Wehrmacht.* By Order of General Keitel the Foreign Ministry was informed on October 5 that *"for military reasons* a common Hungarian-Polish frontier was undesirable." Likewise, "it was . . . *military interest* that Slovakia should not be separated from the Czechoslovak union but should remain with Czechoslovakia under strong German influence." *German Documents,* IV, 40. On October 7 the Director of the Political Department, Wörmann, submitted a policy paper to Hitler in this sense listing alternatives for Slovakia and Ruthenia. The preferred recommendations, accepted by Hitler on October 11, were autonomy for both territories. This the Slovaks already declared, and it was the "most natural solution for the present" in Ruthenia. Both solutions left "other possibilities open," namely an independent Slovakia in the future and a plebiscite in Ruthenia "when time comes." Finally, both solutions could be recognized by Germany under the slogan of "self-determination;" a good slogan not only for the outside world, but also for "rejecting the demands" of Poland and Hungary for solutions to their liking. *German Documents,* IV, 46-49.

[13]*British Documents*, III, 187.

[14]While waiting for the answer Darányi finally managed to tell Hitler that Hungary was now willing to join the Anti-Comintern Pact and to sign an economic agreement with Germany. The atmosphere then improved. Macartney, p. 290.

[15]*German Documents*, IV, 78. For the location of these towns see map attached in *Appendix*.

[16]*Ibid.*

[17]Ciano, *Diary*, October 14.

[18]*German Documents*, IV, 87.

[19]*Ibid.*, p. 89.

[29]*Ibid.*, p. 80. The idea of an Axis arbitration was suggested to the Hungarians earlier by Mussolini.

[21]Macartney, pp. 295, 299.

[22]*Ibid.*, pp. 298-299.

[23]*Supra*, pp. 61-62.

[24]*La Documentation*, p. 29.

[25]*Ibid.*, p. 30.

[26]Ciano, *Diary*, October 15, October 24.

[27]*German Documents*, IV, 83. Cf. L.B. Namier, *Diplomatic Prelude 1938-1939* (London: Macmillan & Co., Ltd., 1948), Chapter II *passim*.

[28]Macartney, p. 299.

[29]*British Documents*, III, 202.

[30]*Ibid.*

[31]*Ibid.*, p. 203.

[32]*La Documentation*, p. 30.

[33]*Ibid.*, pp. 30-31.

[34]*Ibid.*

[35]Ciano, *Diary*, Oct. 22.

[36]*Ibid.*

[37]*Ibid.*

[38]*Ibid.*, Oct. 23

[39]*Ibid.*, Oct. 28.

[40]Ciano, *Diary,* Oct. 28.

[41]*Ibid.*, Oct. 30.

'[2]Ciano, *Diary,* Nov. 3.

[43]*Ibid.*

[44]*German Documents,* IV, 124.

[45]For a detailed description of the pleadings see "Documents on the Vienna Award," *German Documents,* IV, 118-124, reproduced in the *Appendix* here as Document No. 37.

[46]Ciano, *Diary,* Nov. 3. Cf. Erich Kordt, *Nicht aus den Akten...,* (Stuttgart, Union Deutsche Verlagsgesellschafft: 1950), p. 287.

[47]Text of the Award and map showing the frontier established at Vienna are to be found in the *Appendix.*

[48]*British Documents,* III, 238.

[49]Text of the Re-incorporation Bill (Law XXXIV of 1938) is reproduced in Raphael Lemkin, *Axis Rule in Occupied Europe* (Washington: Carnegie Endowment for International Peace, 1944), pp. 361 ff.

[50]*La Documentation,* pp. 33-35.

CHAPTER V

THE LAW AND POLITICS OF THE SETTLEMENT

The review of events presented in the foregoing chapters has revealed certain dominant characteristics of the Czechoslovak-Hungarian dispute and of its settlement. These characteristics have a determining influence on our formulation of the answers to the questions posed at the beginning of this essay.

What were these characteristics?

The first was the absence of any attempt to settle the dispute within the League of Nations.

One should bear in mind here the legal obligations of the parties at the time of the dispute.

The parties were bound by the rules of customary international law. These rules prohibited intervention except in defense, in reprisal, in the support of international law, and in accord with treaty obligations.

Unlike Germany, Hungary never had a Treaty of Arbitration with Czechoslovakia. The disputants were bound, however, by the Pact of Paris of 1928 to seek the settlement of disputes by pacific means. Furthermore, the disputants as well as all other parties interested were, with the exception of Germany, bound by the League Covenant which provided a procedure of collective action for peaceful change.

Article XIX of the Covenant said:

> The Assembly may from time to time advise the consideration by members of the League of treaties which have become inapplicable and the consideration of international conditions whose continuance might endanger the peace of the world.

The League procedure was not invoked by any of the parties directly or indirectly involved.

Nevertheless, neglecting to invoke this procedure could not be considered as a breach of obligations, for the articles of the Covenant did not exclude the possibility of peaceful settlement outside the League framework.

Indeed, the consistent neglect of invoking the League procedure over a period of years, as well as the serious nature of the
dispute, justified recourse to direct negotiations and finally to
arbitration. This method made possible a speedy solution, and it
was not prohibited by international law.

The procedure selected by the parties was viewed in this light
at the time of the dispute. Speaking of the Czechoslovak-Hungarian
negotiations, Viscount Halifax told the House of Commons on
October 24:

> I hope indeed that the rectification of frontiers according to the racial
> distribution of population which is now taking place in Central and South-
> Eastern Europe may contribute to stability and peace. What we are now
> witnessing is the revision of the Treaty of Versailles, for which provision
> was made in the Covenant of the League, but which has never till now
> been made effective.[1]

Was, then, the Vienna Arbitration an instance of peaceful
change, and in accord with international law?

Legal Considerations

During the course of the dispute, as it was seen, pressures
were exercised upon the parties both by each other and by States
whose interests were affected by the issue.

First of all, anxious to avoid another settlement "without her
and against her," Czechoslovakia considered herself pressed by
Point 3 of the Annex to the Munich Agreement, stipulating a
Four Power meeting in the absence of settlement within three
months by agreement between the respective Governments.

Secondly, it appeared that the security of Czechoslovakia
depended, at the time, on German participation in the proposed
international guarantee, which was conditional upon the settlement
of the Polish and Hungarian problems. This fact, too, acted as a
pressure upon the Prague Government.

Furthermore, the Governments of Germany, Italy, and Britain
had frequently intervened both in Prague and in Budapest with
diplomatic representations directed toward influencing the decisions
of the disputants.

Finally, Hungary had irregular forces operating on Czechoslovak territory and, in addition, carried out a partial mobilization
at home.

As we have seen however, the Hungarian Government was
able to disavow itself of the activities of irregulars while maintaining that the partial mobilization was merely a response to
Czechoslovakia's failure to demobilize after the Munich Conference.

If this act of Hungary could be considered as pressure, it was certainly offset by the movement of Czechoslovak troops on or toward the Hungarian border, and by the actions of Rumania and Yugoslavia.

Examining now the use of pressures in international law, it is remarkable that those encountered in the Czechoslovak-Hungarian dispute, as well as the interventions exercised on the diplomatic level, are permissible even today. As Professor Corbett noted in connection with the Annexation of Austria and that of the Sudetenland, "unlike national law, the general 'law of nations' did not invalidate transfers or promises obtained by intimidation."[2]

It is an accepted view in international law, that since there was no personal coercion being exercised against those diplomats who participated in the acts of negotiation and of settlement, the types of pressures exercised upon Czechoslovakia did not affect the peaceful nature and validity of the settlement by arbitral award.

Neither can the absence of Great Britain and France be construed as "further evidence of . . . illegal procedure."[3]

The charge that Czechoslovakia accepted the offer of German-Italian arbitration "under irresistible pressure," and in the face of the "indifference" of the Western Powers, is unwarranted. Prompted by the Slovak leaders, the move to resort to German-Italian arbitration with the issue as a whole came from the Prague Government itself.

As it was seen from the attitude of Great Britain, the Western Powers were willing to take part in an arbitration if so desired by the disputants. As a result, there was no objection raised against the procedure that was selected. As Chamberlain said in the British Parliament on November 14:

> Agreement was, in fact, reached between the Czechoslovak and Hungarian Governments when they agreed to accept as final the arbitral award of the German and Italian Governments, and, in consequence, no question of action by his Majesty's Government arises.[4]

The French seem to have accepted the German explanation, offered by Hitler to the French Ambassador, François-Poncet. Hitler said that by sidetracking Hungary's appeal for a Four Power decision Germany had prevented a possible conflict between the Four Powers and had avoided a "definite danger."[5]

Consequently, the French did not voice disapproval of the arbitration. Although Government documents on the subject are not available, *Le Temps* wrote on November 4 the following:

By the arbitral award the menace of grave complications between Budapest and France is averted and the situation is clarified in the spirit of the Munich Agreement.[6]

There were two additional charges, besides those now considered, brought up against the validity of the settlement by its critics: the legal connection between the Award and the Munich Agreement, and the lack of consent by the Czechoslovak Parliament to the transfer of territory.

In view of the declaration of the Czechoslovak Government to accept in advance the Award as binding, it is hard to see how the lack of parliamentary consent could be held against the validity of the Award.

Finally, as it was pointed out earlier, the Award can not be regarded as a "direct legal consequence of the Munich Agreement." The legal basis of the Award, as it was seen, consisted of the agreement negotiated between Czechoslovakia and Hungary to resort to the arbitral procedure.

One may rightly say, of course, that the settlement of the problem of the Hungarian minority was a "direct political consequence" of the Munich Agreement.

This approach leads to the second important characteristic of the dispute and of its settlement, that is, the supremacy of the political over the legal sphere.

Political Considerations

Throughout the entire dispute there was a conspicuous absence of legal claims and considerations. The dispute was markedly political in its character.

Generally speaking, whenever the arguments of the parties are intended to demonstrate, respectively, that they have title to a territory, the dispute is classified as "legal."[7]

In contrast to the former there are disputes where, instead of trying to prove that they do own, the parties argue that they should be allowed to own the disputed territory. They appeal to considerations outside and above the law. Their claims are economic, strategic, ethnic or historical claims, so-called "non-legal claims to territory."

In the case of the Czechoslovak-Hungarian controversy the issues of the dispute and the scope of the arbitration were, as we had seen, defined through political processes.

Hungary insisted at first not only on ethnographic revision, but also on self-determination for Slovakia and Ruthenia. She derived considerable support from Poland. The main purpose of

Hungary in pursuing this course seems to have been the desire to displace the French-sponsored Little Entente by the weakening of Czechoslovakia.

Poland thought that the annexation of Ruthenia by Hungary would create a common barrier against Germany, remove an important centre for Ukrainian nationalism, and permit the formation of a front against communism.[8]

The weakening of the Little Entente was likewise a purpose of both Germany and of Italy. Germany's chief concern was of course, Czechoslovakia. Willing to see there an ethnic revision, Germany had denied Hungary's larger claims for political and military reasons. Hitler told the Slovak Ministers on March 13, 1939:

> I approved of the Vienna Award in the conviction that the Slovaks would separate themselves from the Czechs and declare their independence, which would be under German protection. That is why I refused Hungarian demands in respect of Slovakia.[9]

Italy on her part pursued a policy of alienating Yugoslavia from the Little Entente, and increasing her own influence in Yugoslavia, as well as in Rumania. This policy had a strong anti-French overtone.

Britain and France, once they consented to the inclusion of the Sudeten Germans into Germany, could not refuse ethnic revision in favor of Hungary.

Finally, the revision on ethnic lines in Czechoslovakia was acceptable to Yugoslavia and Rumania for two reasons. First, neither of them possessed a territory that contained an overwhelmingly Magyar population and at the same time was contiguous with Hungary. Second, with the balance of power having turned in favor of the Axis, both States were eager to show a cooperating attitude.

Thus, while a revision on ethnic lines was thought to result in a more equitable frontier for Hungary, *the selection of the ethnic principle was based primarily on political considerations.*

Political considerations played a part in the selection of the arbitrators as well. The confidence of the Slovak leaders in a decision by Germany in their favor was instrumental in bringing about German-Italian arbitration.[10]

As soon as the larger claims of Hungary had been eliminated and the ethnic principle was accepted, Hungary adjusted herself to the new situation.

After all, her attachment to the Hungarian-inhabited territories of Czechoslovakia was greater than to any other. It was certainly great enough to offer the renunciation of territorial claims to Yugoslavia in exchange of the latter's neutral attitude in the Czechoslovak dispute.[11]

Besides, a revision of this type was still in conformity, if to a lesser extent, with the interests and aims of Hungarian policy. By drawing the frontier on strictly ethnic lines the Hungarian Government hoped to create a situation whereby geographic and economic considerations would, in due course, induce the Ruthenes, and perhaps the Slovaks, to seek re-entry into Hungary.[12]

Once the desirability of the ethnic frontier was established, the main effort of the Hungarian Government was concentrated on excluding all economic considerations from the settlement.

This course of action enjoyed the full support of the Italian and, in the final stage, of the German Governments.

The strict application of the ethnic principle in the Vienna Award was in conspicuous contrast to the application of the principle of self-determination at the Paris Peace Conference of 1919.

On the latter occasion, the principle was, in the delineation of Czechoslovak-Hungarian frontiers, at times severely ignored in favor of economic and strategic considerations, and in general to the disadvantage of Hungary.

The drawing of the frontier well to the south of the ethnic line in Western Slovakia was explained by the necessity of granting Czechoslovakia access to the sea by extending her territory to the Danube River. The line in the central sector was dictated, according to Dr. Beneš, by railway communications.[13]

The latter consideration, supported by the French and the British, took priority over the vital consideration of including the smallest possible number of Magyars within Czechoslovakia, a view advanced by the American and Italian delegates.[14]

Finally, Ruthenia, which was to become an autonomous State within "Czecho-Slovakia," was included in order to provide a common frontier and railway communications with Rumania.[15]

In the end the boundaries of Czechoslovakia, to use the expression of Charles Seymour, American delegate to the conference, did not even "roughly" correspond with the ethnic or linguistic line.[16]

The strict application of the ethnic principle in the Vienna Award produced, however, a frontier, which although more equitable from the ethnic view than that drawn in 1919, was largely unreasonable. The principle of national self-determination was again used as a principle of disintegration.[17]

64

R.W. Seton-Watson noted the following:

> For the restoration of the Danube island and the district around Nové
> Zámky and Levice, where the population is overwhelmingly Magyar, a
> good case could be made out, though it meant cutting off Slovakia from
> access to the Danube, save for a few kilometres to the east of Bratislava.
> On a purely ethnographic basis the Magyars were entitled to recover the
> towns of Rimavská Sobota and Rožnava, though the result has been to
> render communications by road and rail impossible along the whole south-
> ern border of Slovakia. But by the cession of Košice Slovakia had been
> deprived of its second capital, the natural and only possible economic and
> cultural centre of the whole eastern half of Slovak territory; and this was
> done on the basis of the census of 1910.[18]

The province Ruthenia was deprived of its two principal
towns, Ungvár and Munkács, and of the whole of its fertile territory, without which she was practically unable to exist. Ruthenia
retained in fact only the mountainous region in the north, while
its system of communications with Slovakia had been completely
dislocated.[19]

Without doubt, the ethnic principle had been interpreted
"generously in Hungary's favor."[20]

The noted expert on East-Central Europe, Hugh Seton-Watson
remarked that "the frontier between Hungary and Slovakia could
be drawn on lines more generous to Hungary than 1920 while less
unfair to the Slovaks than 1938."[21]

True, those who criticized the Vienna Award on substance
rather than on procedure were on safe ground. Legal criticisms are
not only invalid but also largely irrelevant, for it is clear that the
settlement of the dispute was a political rather than a legal act.
The fact that the political process was mitigated in the end by
recourse to arbitral procedure did not alter the outstanding political nature of the settlement.[22]

It is only because international law recognizes, besides judicial
settlements, the acts of negotiation, conciliation, and mediation
as falling under pacific settlement that we may consider the
Vienna Award as falling within the sphere of international law.
Viewed in this broader sense, it was an instance of peaceful change,
valid at its time under international law. For, imperfect as it may
have been, the settlement had its advantages.

In international society there are at present, two modes existing for change: by grace of the States affected and by war. Of the
two methods the first is by far the more desirable, even though it
takes the aspects of a sort of "international collective bargaining,"
as was the case in the settlement of the Czechoslovak-Hungarian
dispute.

The Status of the Award

For some time after its rendering, the Award was sustained by all parties directly or indirectly involved.

Speaking on the subject in the House of Commons on December 19, 1938, Chamberlain said that since agreement had been reached between Czechoslovakia and Hungary on the problem of the new frontier, "the question of the conclusion of a further international instrument regarding these frontiers does not appear to arise."[23]

The Hungarian Minister, Barcza, inquired in the British Foreign Office whether this, as well as the previous declaration of the Prime Minister could be taken as *de jure* recognition of the Vienna Award. He received a verbal answer in the affirmative.[24] Later the British Government gave what amounted to *de facto* recognition by extending the powers of its Consul in Budapest to the recovered area.

The Hungarian Government, however, failed to take the precaution of getting written confirmation of the recognition. Macartney noted in this connection:

> Nevertheless, it is hard for an Englishman not to blush when he reads the Foreign Office's argument, delivered on 30th January, 1941, that Great Britain was not bound by the Vienna Award because it had not been reached in accordance with the procedure laid down at Munich, but represented the result of a decision by two of the Munich Powers only, who had not consulted the other two.[25]

The French position at the time of the arbitration was, as we had seen, similar to that of the British.

Germany and Italy on their part were quite anxious to have the validity of the Award observed by Czechoslovakia and by Hungary. When the latter had, in November 1938, begun to plan military action for the recovery of the rest of Ruthenia under the pretext of protecting persecuted Hungarians, both Berlin and Rome protested in most emphatic terms, enjoining the Hungarian Government to respect the Vienna decision.[26]

As in the case of the Munich Agreement, the Soviet Government maintained silence on the question. Yet, after the conclusion of the German-Soviet Pact in August, 1939, Moscow formally recognized the then independent Slovakia. This act implied the recognition of the latter's frontiers as set by the Vienna Award.

The first violation of the terms of the Award was committed, according to the Czechoslovak view, by Hungary when she occupied Ruthenia on March 15, 1939. On the preceding day, as it is known, Slovakia declared herself independent, and Germany occupied Bohemia and Moravia to establish a "protectorate."

The Hungarian view was, of course, that Czechoslovakia having ceased to exist, Hungary was not bound any longer by the Vienna Award. At the same time Chamberlain regarded the declaration of Slovak independence as "an end by internal disruption" of Czechoslovakia.[27]

The ensuing application for, and granting of, consular *exequatur* between Slovakia, Germany, Great Britain, France, the United States, and others, indicate that there was, indeed, a *de facto* recognition of the new status of the former Czechoslovak territories.

On the request of the Czechoslovak Government-in-Exile during the war the British had, on August 5, 1942, declared that "at the final settlement of the Czechoslovak frontiers to be reached at the end of the war they will not be influenced by any changes effected in and since 1938."

Whether the above fact constituted a recognition of Czechoslovakia's pre-Munich frontier is debatable.

The French National Committee of Liberation went farther. In a letter to the Czechoslovak Government General De Gaulle expressly repudiated on September 29, 1942, the Munich Agreement by considering it, as well as all acts accomplished in the application thereof, as "nuls et nonavenues." [28]

As for the Soviet Union, her agreement with the Czechoslovak Provisional Government concluded on July 18, 1941, constituted, in Táborsky's view, a recognition of the pre-Munich legal situation of Czechoslovakia.[29]

Factually the terms of the Vienna Award were annulled in the winter of 1944 by the Red Army and by subsequent handing over of the administration of those territories to Czechoslovak authorities.

De jure the Award was repudiated by the Paris Peace Treaties of 1947. Thereby the pre-Munich frontier between Slovakia and Hungary was restored. Ruthenia, however, was ceded by Czechoslovakia to the Soviet Union.

At present, silence reigns over the question of the Czechoslovak-Hungarian territorial controversy. Influenced by Moscow, the Communist Governments of the two countries seem to have accepted the *status quo*. This much, at least, is known in the case of Hungary where Joseph Révai, the well known party-ideologist, denounced the ethnic principle as early as April 28, 1946.

A more recent position was voiced by Béla Bellér, an expert on the question of nationalities. According to him the "socialist solution," conforming equally to the interest of the minority and the majority, will "minimize" and "gradually eliminate" the question of nationality and territory.[30]

The temporary success of the Hungarian revolution in October 1956 raised in some minds the question, what would be the attitude of a non-Communist Government in Hungary toward the neighboring States still possessing a considerable number of Hungarians?

From the official pronouncements of Government spokesmen it appeared that the new Hungarian Government interpreted its declared policy of neutrality without discriminating against neighbor States.

On November 1, 1956, Prime Minister Imre Nagy reaffirmed in the Budapest radio Hungary's desire to live in "true friendship" with her neighbors.[31]

On the same day "Rádió Miskolc," sponsored by the Workers' Council of Borsod County, broadcasted in the Slovak language a commentary on events in Hungary. Besides pointing out that the fight of the previous days was by no means a counter-revolution, the program reaffirmed: "We do not proclaim revisionist slogans, we do not want a frontier revision."[32]

On November 3, Cardinal Mindszenty warned his listeners over the Budapest radio of the necessity of a revaluation of the old-type nationalism so as to prevent its becoming a source of friction among nations.[33]

Nevertheless, barely two weeks after the suppression of the revolt by Soviet troops the new Communist leader of Hungary, János Kádár, made a statement to the Pravda of Moscow, voicing an entirely different view.

Among others, Kádár expressed his thanks to the Soviet Union for preventing in Hungary the coming into existence of a "warmongering" attitude. In his opinion, the victory of the "counter-revolutionaries" would have resulted in immediate armed attack upon the neighbor States to recover lost territories.[34]

It is left to the reader to decide which of the two opposing views appears to represent the true position of the Hungarian people on the question.

The Future

As it was mentioned before, the Paris Peace Treaties of 1947 declared the decisions of the Vienna Award "null and void." By this provision the status of the Award had been definitely settled. Nevertheless, the question of the Czechoslovak-Hungarian dispute did not go undiscussed during the peace negotiations. As a matter of fact, the result of the discussions and of the events that took place after the conclusion of the Treaty of Peace indicate that the question may once again come up in the future.

Speaking of the negotiations of 1947 it is necessary to keep in mind that the central issues of the Peace Conference were not the adjustment of frontiers here and there, but the questions of Germany and Russia.

In the treatment of these issues considerations of strategy, power, and prestige were paramount. The chief concern of the Allied Powers turned out to be the location of the dividing line between the West and Russia. East of the dividing line, the Western Powers did not show too much inclination to press for "ethnic lines" and for "fair solutions."[35]

Even where they did, political opportunism prevailed. This was particularly true when it came to disputes between Allied and enemy States. Here the problem was difficult for political reasons.

Examining the American preparations for the peace negotiations, Campbell noted the following:

> If long term stability in this region was the American purpose, there was something to be said for avoiding, in territorial disputes, the ideas of rewarding our allies and penalizing our enemies. This would mean, for example . . . favoring Hungary's claim to the solidly Magyar populated territory just across the frontier in Czechoslovakia. No firm decision was ever taken in Washington on this point. To suggest to allied states that they give up territory was too high a political hurdle to jump—especially while the war was on. The immediate disadvantages were apparent; the long term benefits were intangible.[36]

The Czechoslovak-Hungarian question was brought up at the Conference by the Czechs themselves in the form of a demand for five Hungarian villages opposite Bratislava to enlarge their bridgehead on that side of the Danube, and by seeking international sanctions for their plan to transfer by force 200,000 of their Magyar minority to Hungary. About 100,000 other Hungarians were expected to be exchanged on a voluntary basis, and the remainder were to be "re-Slovakized."

Hungarian spokesmen seized the opportunity to point out that "the easiest way to dispose of the Hungarian minority was to dispose also of the land on which it lived."[37]

In view of the Hungarian opposition to the Czechoslovak proposal of population transfer, the representatives of Australia contended that "it would be wrong to attempt to write into this treaty a clause permitting a forced transfer, against the wishes of the receiving country."[38]

69

The American and British delegations did not sympathize with the Czech proposals, but were willing to consider them in connection with a general settlement of Czechoslovak-Hungarian differences. In the American view, an exchange of territory satisfying Czechoslovakia's desire opposite Bratislava and giving Hungary part of the overwhelmingly Hungarian populated territory along the border would have reduced the scope of population transfer.

This solution, however, was impossible without the cooperation of the Soviets. The Czechs on their part resented the idea of treating Hungary as an equal and chose to have their case discussed by the Conference rather than to make a backstage deal desired by Hungary.[39]

In the final solution Czechoslovakia was given three villages opposite Bratislava, and the question of population transfer was postponed by obliging Hungary to enter into negotiations with Czechoslovakia to solve the remaining problems. Ultimately the two Governments were unable to reach an agreement. The result was a mass expulsion of Hungarians from Czechoslovakia.

It still remains to be seen whether this action constituted a final settlement of the problem. Yet, it is unlikely that the Czechoslovak-Hungarian dispute was put to rest indefinitely by means of a forced population transfer.

At the same time we may note that the turning over of the minority problem to the parties least likely to find a mutually satisfactory solution was, in effect, "an evasion of responsibility of the Powers charged with negotiating peace treaties."[40]

Here as a concluding note we may mark the crucial role which the Great Powers have played and will continue to play in the destiny of East-Central Europe.

It is true that the differential treatment of peoples, practiced both during the days of the Hapsburg Monarchy and after the First World War, can be eliminated in this region to some extent through the efforts of the peoples themselves concerned. Yet, the main conditions necessary for establishing the principle of equal treatment are outside conditions: the absence of domination of the area by one Great Power (or Power Bloc), as well as the absence of rivalry of two or more Great Powers (Power Blocs) projecting itself into this area.

Plans and suggestions for "federation" as a solution of the territorial problems are purely theoretical. To speak of "federation" is illusory until its main condition, a more stable order in Europe, has been established. The experience of the League period, just as that of the United Nations, shows that the rule of law in a given period can not be stronger than the structure of relationships among the Great Powers that underlies it.

In the modern view "law is a function of a given political order whose existence alone can make it binding."[41]

Assuming this to be true—a view shared by the writer of this essay—it is evident that the establishment of the required order, on which the rule of law in East-Central Europe can rest, is a political task.

Ultimately then, the final settlement and eventual elimination of the Czechoslovak-Hungarian dispute will have to be achieved by international politics, and not by international law.

Notes to Chapter V

[1]H.H.E. Craster, (ed.), *Speeches on Foreign Policy by Viscount Halifax*, (London: Oxford University Press, 1940), p. 204.

[2]P.E. Corbett, *Law and Society in the Relations of States*, (New York: Harcourt, Brace and Co., 1951), p. 120.

[3]Cf. *Supra*, p. 7, n. 15.

[4]Parliament, Great Britain, *Parliamentary Debates*. House of Commons, Fifth Series, (London: His Majesty's Stationary Office, 1938-1939), Vol. 341, p. 477, col. 1.

[5]Ministére des Affaires Étrangères, France, *The French Yellow Book, Diplomatic Documents 1938-1939*, (London: Hutchinson and Co., Ltd., 1940), p. 25.

[6]Quoted by Macartney, p. 303.

[7]In international practice the following titles are recognized by States: occupation, accretion, prescription, cession, and conquest. They are called "legal claims" to territory. Cf. Charles Fenwick, *International Law* (3rd ed.; New York: Appleton, 1954), p. 343.

[8]*British Documents*, III, 181.

[9]International Military Tribunal, *Trial of the Major War Criminals Before the International Military Tribunal*, Vol. XXXV (Nuremberg: I.M.T., 1949), p. 175.

[10]This was confirmed recently. Cf. Jozef Lettrich, *History of Modern Slovakia* (New York: Praeger, 1955), p. 103.

[11]*Documents Secrets*, II, 22, 33, 37.

[12]*Survey*, III, 70.

[13]Francis Deak, *Hungary at the Paris Peace Conference* (New York: Columbia University Press, 1942), pp. 28, 35, 36.

[14]*Deak*, p. 45.

[15]*Ibid.*, pp. 35, ff.

[16]E.M. House and C. Seymour, *What Really Happened at Paris?* (New York: Charles Scribner's Sons, 1921), p. 103.

[17]Alfred Cobban, *National Self-Determination* (Chicago: University of Chicago Press, 1947), p. 42.

[18]R.W. Seton-Watson, *From Munich to Danzig*, (London: Methuen & Co., 1939), pp. 116-117.

[19]Ripka, pp. 202, 204.

[20]Elisabeth Wiskemann, *Prologue to War* (London: Oxford University Press, 1945), p. 21.

[21]Hugh Seton-Watson, *Eastern Europe Between the Wars, 1918-1941* (Cambridge: The University Press, 1945), p. 349.

[22]Ross classified it as "political arbitration of binding character." Alf Ross, *Textbook of International Law* (London: Longmans, Green & Co., 1947), p. 274.

[23]*Parliamentary Debates*, H. of C., Vol. 342, p. 2460.

[24]Macartney, p. 303.

[25]*Ibid.*

[26]*British Documents*, III, 236.

[27]*Parliamentary Debates*, H. of C., Vol. 345, p. 437.

[28]Taborsky, *Czechoslovak Cause*, p. 26.

[29]*Ibid.*, p. 99.

[30]"Idézetek, Vélemények és Nyilatkozatok," *Bulletin of the Research Institute for Minority Studies on Hungarians* (New York): II (July-September 1957), 23.

[31]László Varga, ed., "A Magyar Forradalom és Szabadságharc," *Magyarországi Események*, VIII (1956 Október-23-November 9), 270.

[32]Varga, p. 289.

[33]*Ibid.*, p. 343.

[34]"Idézetek, Vélemények ...," *Bulletin of the Research Institute for Minority Studies on Hungarians*, II, 25.

[35]Campbell, pp. 199-201.

[36]Campbell, p. 198.

[37] *Ibid.*, p. 213.

[38] I.L. Claude, Jr., *National Minorities* (Cambridge: Harvard University Press, 1955), p. 132, quoting *Hungary and the Conference of Paris* (Budapest: Hungarian Ministry for Foreign Affairs, 1947), IV, 101.

[39] "Who won this war," asked Jan Masaryk in one of his speeches to the Conference, "the United Nations or Hungary?" Campbell, p. 213.

[40] Campbell, p. 214.

[41] E.H. Carr, *The Twenty Years' Crisis*, 1919-1939 (2d. ed., London: Macmillan & Co., Ltd.), p. 178.

EPILOGUE

In the Spring of 1968 the peoples of Czechoslovakia succeeded in freeing themselves from the domestic Stalinist leadership and established a new regime under Alexander Dubček. Among the numerous changes which began to take place, there was one affecting the Hungarian minority. The American daily paper, *The Christian Science Monitor*, reported in its June 20, 1968, issue the following:

> The New Czechoslovakia is openly airing a topic which for years has been kept quietly under the rug—its national minorities.
>
> Some 650,000 Hungarians, 110,000 Germans, and smaller numbers of Poles and Ukrainians live within Czechoslovakia's borders.
>
> As long as the Communists were running things, they gave the impression that this problem of national minorities, which had vexed Eastern and Southeastern Europe before World War II, had virtually vanished under their regime.
>
> Now the "Cultural Association of Hungarian Workers in Czechoslovakia" has presented to the government a series of demands. Its members want full equality and limited national self-government.
>
> President Svoboda and the Central Committee of the Czechoslovak party both acknowledge the validity of these claims. And they have indicated that other minorities also will be made to feel at home in Czechoslovakia.

Already on March 15, 1968, the Slovak National Council (Slovenská Národná Rada) came out strongly for the concept of federalism, the right of self-determination, and sovereignty in relation to the two state-forming nations, the Czechs and the Slovaks. The Council's declaration also promised to create legal and political conditions insuring the economic and cultural development of Hungarian and Ukrainian nationalities in Slovakia.

Moving toward the transformation of Czechoslovakia into a federal political system, the reform movement took several constructive steps by promising to re-establish the rights of nationalities and putting emphasis on the question of political representation of national minorities.

Unfortunately, before these plans could be implemented, Soviet and Warsaw Pact troops invaded and occupied Czechoslovakia, adding one more instance to the long list of Great Power interventions in East Central Europe.

In the end, the impending law on federalization was passed by the non-democratic, dogmatic Communist party leadership which came to power by the grace of the Soviet Union. According to Chapter I, Article 1, Paragraph 4 of Constitutional Law No. 143 (October 27, 1968) the Socialist Republic of Czechoslovakia consists of two components: the Czech Socialist Republic and the Slovak Socialist Republic. Lip service has been paid in the Preamble to the idea of recognizing the nationalities as constituting elements, but the implementation of the idea is totally missing. Nationalities as collective entities have no rights whatsoever, only individuals do.

Less than three years after the constitutional changes eleven members of the U.S. Congress—including the later President Gerald Ford—saw it fit to voice their concern on the floor of the House of Representatives about the worsening situation of the Hungarian minority in Czechoslovakia under the neo-Stalinist leadership imposed on the country. Together, the American Hungarian Federation (Washington, D.C.) and the National Committee of Hungarians in Czechoslovakia (Cleveland, Ohio), in a Resolution inserted in the *Congressional Record* on July 20, 1971, by Congressman Patten of New Jersey, expressed their concern that "the continuing deterioration of the cultural and political rights of the Hungarians in Czechoslovakia may be a consequence of Soviet policy to rekindle some support in Slovakia by giving free reign to Slovak antagonisms toward Hungarians as a concession for forcing upon the Slovaks the occupation of their country."

There is evidence, indeed, that the Soviet Union—like other Great Powers before—is using the "divide and rule" tactics to maintain its domination in the East Central European area. The persecution of Hungarians in Transylvania under the Ceausescu regime in Romania has recently reached such proportions that the Hungarian government deemed it necessary to lodge an official protest. Reports from Czechoslovakia indicate that discrimination against nationalities has been extended to include even Slovaks, who belong to one of the "constituting nations." In a memorandum dated February 2, 1978, and addressed to the governments participating in the Belgrade Conference (a follow-up to the Helsinki Conference on European Security), the Slovak World Congress complained that the Slovak minority in the Czech Socialist Republic has been left without Slovak schools, except for a few elementary schools, without cultural associations and institutions, without newspapers and has no means to face the assimilation policy of the Prague government.

The above complaint, datelined from Toronto, Ontario (Canada), makes it easier to understand the concern voiced earlier by the National Committee of Hungarians in Czechoslovakia about the changes that occurred in the Cultural Association of Hungarian Workers in Czechoslovakia, known by its acronym as CSEMADOK. Referring to the developments which followed the replacement of Dubček by Gustáv Husák, the N.C.H.C. reported that "the only nationwide organization of the Hungarians, in Slovakia, the CSEMADOK, was taken over by the representatives of the Czechoslovak Communist Party. The liberal-minded young Hungarians who were elected to the leadership of CSEMADOK during the Dubček era were purged by the newly "co-opted" members imposed upon them by the Party. "This change removed the only organization of Hungarians in Slovakia as a political and cultural force."

In the same statement, inserted in the *U.S. Congressional Record* by Representative Ashbrook on July 20, 1971, the N.C.H.C. issued a call:

> We call the attention of the Free World to discern and learn from the bitter experience of neo-Stalinism which the almost one million Hungarians of Slovakia are undergoing and the Free World should recognize, too, the necessity for a new settlement in Central Europe.

Has the time come for a new settlement, or at least a reassessment of the question of nationalities in East Central Europe?

Without doubt, the contention of the Soviet-inspired communist parties, namely that the problem of national minorities can be solved by adherence to "socialist internationalism," has turned out to be completely unfounded. Historians in the Soviet-dominated countries, who accepted the party directives in the 1950's on how to write history, are beginning to discover that the problem of national minorities can no longer be "kept quietly under the rug." As a result, some of them are re-evaluating the approach, as well as the problem itself. To believe in "automatism," the idea that once socialism has been consolidated the problem of national minorities would solve itself, is now considered outmoded. Instead, emphasis is put on non-economic and non-political factors, such as "trust" between nations and nationalities.

Lamentably, this "trust" in Czechoslovakia between the Slovaks and the Hungarians is absent, if it ever has been there.

Not even the actual number of Hungarians may be known for sure. The 1970 census recorded 621,588 persons who declared Hungarian as their mother tongue. Of these 21,339 lived in the Czech Socialist Republic, the remaining 600,249 in the Slovak

Socialist Republic. Of the total number 570,478 claimed Hungarian as their nationality. By the end of 1974 this number had risen to 583,000.

However, the reliability of these figures remains doubtful in the light of what happened earlier. The 1950 census recorded only 354,532 persons of Hungarian nationality. By 1961 the number had risen to 518,782, a feat that could be explained only by assuming—as a Slovak politician put it with wry humor—that Hungarian mothers in Slovakia must have given birth three times a year between these two dates. What is more likely is that the 1950 records were, for one reason or other (there are several possible explanations), a distortion of reality.

The 1977 edition of the Hungarian Encyclopedia of Ethnography (Budapest) estimates the number of Hungarians in Czechoslovakia—cautiously—at 700,000 to 730,000.

Adding to this the estimated 500,000 Hungarians in Yugoslavia, and 2,500,000 or so in Rumania, one may indeed conclude that the nationality problem, created by the Paris Peace Treaties, still exists, and that the time may be near when a redefinition of the right of self-determination and a rethinking of the problem of national minorities will become absolutely necessary.

APPENDIX

DOCUMENTS
MAPS

DIPLOMATIC CORRESPONDENCE

CONCERNING THE VIENNA AWARD

1.

760F.62/419

The Minister in Hungary (Montgomery) to the Secretary of State[1]

No. 1084   Budapest, June 2, 1938

(Received June 14.)

Sir: I have the honor to inform the Department that in a conversation with Dr. Tibor Eckhardt a few nights ago I told him that I was giving considerable thought as to

(1) whether there is any agreement between the Hungarian Government and the German Government with regard to Czechoslovakia,

(2) whether Hungary will attempt to send its Army into Slovakia should the Germans enter Bohemia,

and that although Mr. de Kánya had repeatedly given me assurances, I still wondered whether there was not some secret understanding, the knowledge of which was being withheld from me. I thereupon asked Dr. Eckhardt frankly if he would tell me the real truth. Dr. Eckhardt assured me that there was no secret understanding of any kind, that he had discussed this question with the Regent, Prime Minister Imrédy, and Foreign Minister de Kánya and that it was the agreed policy that Hungary would remain completely neutral in the event of a war and would take no action towards Czechoslovakia that would disturb the peace of Europe. Dr. Eckhardt further told me that this policy was based upon the following three points:

---

[1] *U.S. Foreign Relations 1938, I. 55-56.*

(1) Yugoslavia and Rumania are bound under the Little Entente agreement to aid Czechoslovakia in case of attack by Hungary, and Yugoslavia in particular is not averse to taking over some Hungarian territory should the occasion therefor arise;

(2) Hungary cannot afford to go into any war and desires to remain neutral. To act in conjunction with Germany would make her an ally of that country, which would be extremely dangerous, and if war resulted Hungary would be dragged into it;

(3) In case of the breaking up of Czechoslovakia, Slovakia would naturally return to Hungary. Poland desires a common frontier with Hungary and would use every influence to that end. If Hungary does not disturb the peace of Europe her chances of getting back some of its lost provinces are better than if she involved herself at the start.

A few days after my conversation with Dr. Eckhardt a member of the staff of the Legation called on Baron Apor and questioned him on the same subjects and he, like de Kánya, denied that there is any agreement between the Hungarian and German Governments, stating that "the moment Hungary made any agreement with any large power, from that day on Hungary would be dominated by that power," and then added most emphatically, "No, Hungary must make no agreements, we must play a lone hand."

I am convinced that the above represents the present policy of the Hungarian Government and that unless pressure of public opinion forces it to do otherwise, or there should be some change in the Government, it will not take any hasty or ill considered action.

Respectfully yours,

John F. Montgomery

2.

Joint Communiqué Concerning the Bled Agreement Between the Little Entente and Hungary, August, 23, 1938.[1]

The negotiations which have been in progress since last year between Hungary on the one hand and Rumania, Yugoslavia, and Czechoslovakia on the other, and which were inspired by the common desire to rid their mutual relations of everything which could impede the development of good neighbourliness between Hungary and these three States, have resulted in provisional agreements. These agreements include the recognition by the three States of the Little Entente of Hungary's equality of rights as regards armament, as well as the mutual renunciation of

---

[1]*Doc. Int. Affairs 1938, I. 284.*

any recourse to force between Hungary and the States of the Little Entente.

During the conversations which preceded this agreement, all questions the solution of which might favourably affect relations between the Danube States were discussed in detail and in a friendly spirit. It has been intended to issue declarations embodying the views of the above-mentioned countries on these questions. It was not, however, possible to draw up these declarations in final form. It is hoped that when these difficulties have been overcome, the negotiations will be successfully concluded, and that the completed agreements and the above-mentioned declarations will be published simultaneously.

3.

F18-371-374

**Minute by the State Secretary (Weizsäcker)
for the Foreign Minister's Secretariat.**[1]

Secret   On Board "Patria," August 23, 1938

While the Führer and the Hungarian Regent discussed political matters on the morning of August 23, the Hungarian Ministers Imrédy and Kánya were closeted with Herr von Ribbentrop. Herr von Weizsäcker was also present during this conversation. M. Kánya brought forward two subjects:

(1) The Hungarian negotiations with the Little Entente and
(2) The Czech problem.

Kánya's observations on point (1), negotiations with the Little Entente, were mainly historical and produced actually nothing new. In any case, they were insufficient to justify any addition to the closing communiqué, which Kánya laid on the table. This communiqué is due to be issued today by the conference of the Little Entente. It appears that Baron Apor, in Budapest, and Bessenyi, Minister in Belgrade, have agreed to it. The question whether it was opportune was therefore really out of date. Nevertheless, one must go more deeply into it to bring out the German point of view.

Herr von Ribbentrop explained how, in his opinion, the renunciation of the use of force, which is to be proclaimed afresh, would not have the desired political effect, namely, that of protecting Hungary from Yugoslavia, particularly in the event of a Hungarian-Czech crisis. On the

---

[1]*German Documents*, II, 609 ff.

contrary, Hungary was blocking the road to intervention in Czechoslovakia and making it more difficult morally for the Yugoslavs to leave their Czech allies in the lurch. The impartial reader will say to himself that Hungary is moving away from the German-Czech political conflict and, in effect, renouncing revision, since he who does not assists departs with empty hands.

Kánya's arguments against this were unconvincing. They all touched on point 2, namely Hungary's attitude in the event of a German-Czech conflict.

Herr von Ribbentrop asked the Hungarians how they would act if the Führer put into effect his decision of replying by the use of force to any new Czech provocation. The Hungarians hedged on two points: Yugoslavia must remain neutral if Hungary were to march northward and, eventually, to the east. Moreover, Hungarian re-armament had only just started and would require another year or two to complete.

To this Herr von Ribbentrop remarked to the Hungarians that the Yugoslavs would take care not to walk into the pincers of the Axis Powers. Rumania, too, would certainly not move on her own. England and France would likewise remain quiescent. England would not lightly risk the loss of the Empire, for she appreciates our newly recovered strength. It is not possible, however, to say anything definite in advance concerning the exact time of the event we are considering, since this depends on Czech provocation. Herr von Ribbentrop repeated that those who desired revision must seize opportunity by the forelock and themselves take an active part. Thus the Hungarian reply still remained subject to conditions.

As to Herr von Ribbentrop's question, what object the desired conversations between the General Staffs supposed to have, little emerged save the Hungarian wish for a kind of mutual military inventory and preparatory stocktaking for the Czech conflict. No definite political basis for this — the exact moment for Hungarian intervention — was agreed.

Meanwhile, Horthy had expressed himself to the Führer in more definite language. While not keeping silent on his misgivings as to the British attitude, he nevertheless made it clear that Hungary intended to co-operate. The Hungarian Ministers were and still remain more skeptical, for they realize more strongly the direct danger to Hungary's unprotected flanks.

M. Imrédy had an interview with the Führer in the afternoon and was most relieved when the Führer stated to him that, in this particular case, he required nothing of Hungary. He himself did not know the precise moment. He who wanted to sit at table must at least help in the kitchen. If Hungary desired General Staff conversations, he had no objections.

The Hungarian point of view can quite well be summarized today as follows: (a) Hungary is glad at not having to expect from us demands in the form of an ultimatum, and (b) Hungary is convinced that she will not be able to intervene until some 14 days after the out-break of war.

Weizsäcker

4.

F18/369-370

Minute by the State Secretary (Weizsäcker)[1]

Berlin, August 25, 1938

Today the Reich Minister had a further conversation with M. Kánya, at the latter's request. The Reich Minister pointed out to M. Kánya the jubilation of the Czech, French, and British press over the Bled communiqué and repeated that this event, especially at the present moment, was regarded abroad as a rift in German-Hungarian friendship and as a renunciation by Hungary of her revisionist aims. M. Kánya again put forward the already well known points of view on the legal situation and on the questionable value of the so-called preliminary agreements between Hungary and the Little Entente, and in particular tried once more to prove that the intensified Hungarian demands on Czechoslovakia for protection of the minorities ensure that the agreement will never be fulfilled. And even if it were fulfilled, said M. Kánya, it would never be kept by the other side, and so Hungary would be freed from the observance of her guarantee not to use force. M. Kánya is expecting more detailed information from Budapest as to how far they have actually got with the initialing of the treaties, and will inform the Reich Minister on this. The Reich Minister and M. Kánya agreed that a great deal depended on the treatment of the Bled Communiqué in the Hungarian press during the coming weeks.

With reference to Hungary's willingness to take an active part in the event of a German-Czech conflict, it is known that M. Kánya said a few days ago that an interval of one to two years was necessary in order to develop Hungary's fighting forces sufficiently. In today's conversation, M. Kánya amended this remark by saying that Hungary's military strength had in fact improved. By October 1 this year their armament would be so far advanced as to enable them to take part.

Weizsäcker

---

[1]*German Documents*, II. 623-624.

85

Conversation of the Polish Ambassador in Berlin, Józef Lipski, with General Field Marshal Göring[1]

August 24, 1938

(excerpts)   Strictly Confidential

(. . .)

Göring remarked that he had not yet had an occasion to talk with Regent Horthy and his staff, who will only arrive in Berlin this afternoon. He wanted to stress that the German government exerted pressure on Budapest to conduct negotiations so as to avoid collective obligations with the states of the Little Entente but to enter into agreement separately with Belgrade and Bucharest, omitting Prague. Göring remarked that Stoyadinovich followed the line of these suggestions at the Bled conference (if I understood correctly). Thus, in Göring's opinion, Hungary would be free to act, as he put it, in the last stage, its action anticipated to follow only a few days after that of the Germans. Göring described Hungary's stand as somewhat soft *(flau)*.

(. . .)

Returning to the Czech problem, Göring cited the British opinion that in a matter of time everything could be settled. He does not share that opinion. He cannot conceive how the Czechs could agree to any concessions, since their state is composed of so many nationalities. For instance, if in order to make things even with Poland they would grant it all concessions, then similar concessions would have to be made to all other minorities. Therefore, the situation is at an impasse.

Following your instructions, I replied to these declarations that we also do not believe the present Czech creation can exist any longer. Nor do we see any change in Czech policy. I added that of late efforts have been made to draw us into anti-German deals but that the Polish government rejected these offers categorically. I ascertained that international propaganda presents German policy as pushing ever new claims and provoking conflicts. Poland, I added, does not believe this. Here Göring reacted very strongly, saying that indeed propaganda imputes to Germany intentions of new territorial demands . . .

I returned to the Hungarian problem. I stressed Polish-Hungarian friendship, describing Hungary as an element of stabilization in the Danubian basin. Referring to the expression Göring used earlier—that

---

[1]Waclaw Jedrzejewicz (ed.), *Diplomat in Berlin 1933-1939. Papers and Memoirs of Józef Lipski, Ambassador of Poland* (New York: Columbia University Press, 1968), pp. 382-86. Hereafter cited as *Lipski Papers*.

the Hungarians are a bit *flau*—I came out with the question whether, in his opinion, they are mature enough for independent action. I remarked that the untimely death of Gömbös[2] was a heavy loss of Hungary. Göring confirmed my opinion, as well as my judgement that still not enough understanding might be observed in Hungarian statesmen on nationality problems *(völkisch)*.

In discussion on this item, important opinions of Göring are worth noting. First of all, he remarked that Germany has no precise understanding on this matter with Hungary, nor does it have any with Poland. On the other hand, Germany is aware of Hungary's interests in Czechoslovakia, and the same relates to Poland. The Germans envisaged that, in case Germany undertook any action, Hungary would join. Germany is taking on itself the task of restraining Belgrade from acting against Hungary. It expects that Warsaw would act along the same lines toward Bucharest in order to prevent any action. It would be most embarrassing if Hungary did not make a move, since Czech forces could then retreat to Slovakia. Evidently, Germany would not demand military assistance from Budapest or Warsaw, if only for the reason that this would look derisory in view of Germany's predominance over Czechoslovakia. But Germany understands that under such circumstances Poland would occupy the region of interest to it. In practice it might occur that Polish and German units would meet somewhere.

In connection with these deliberations of Göring, I stressed that Poland is closely united with Slovakia, owing to links of race and language. The ties are even closer since we have no claims to Slovakia. I observed that the evolution of the Slovak nation had progressed rapidly, especially in the last years, and I said that it is imperative that Slovakia be granted autonomy from either one side or the other—from the Czechs or the Hungarians.

Göring eagerly confirmed that this is a necessity. He added that Germany is fortunately in such a position that these matters are of no concern to it. On the other hand, there is the question of relations between Warsaw and Budapest, and Poland's good influence on Hungary. In his opinion Hungary should grant the autonomy which was refused by Czechoslovakia.

With regard to Sub-Carpathian Russia I observed, following instructions, that it is a place where international intrigues abound, adding that this land was taken away from Hungary solely for the purpose of giving Czechoslovakia access to Russia . . .

Józef Lipski

---

[2]Julius Gömbös, the Hungarian prime minister, died on October 6, 1935.

6.

1863/423026
Unsigned Foreign Ministry Minute for the Foreign Minister[1]

Berlin, September 26, 1938

(Pol. IV 6621)

The Rumanian Minister in Rome has given, in the name of his Government, the following secret information to the Italian Foreign Minister:

(1) Rumania is being subjected to very heavy pressure to allow transit rights to Soviet troops in the event of German attack on Czechoslovakia. Rumania has emphatically refused to grant this request.

(2) Rumania fully appreciates Hungary's hopes of regaining the areas which once were hers and now belong to Prague. In the name of his Government, the Rumanian Minister requested the Italian Government to exert their influence in Budapest so as to prevent any impulsive action which might make the international situation more difficult for Rumania, especially with respect to the treaties of the Little Entente. Lastly, Rumania pointed out that her attitude would have to be reconsidered if Hungary increased her demands to include areas which did not contain Hungarian populations.

Minister Ciano replied to M. Zamfirescu that the alliances of the Little Entente must be considered as dissolved, in view of the substantial changes in the status of one of the signatories. The Italian Foreign Minister also inquired what attitude Rumania would adopt in the event of a Polish-Soviet conflict. The Rumanian Minister answered that without doubt Rumania would take the side of Warsaw and that, in any case, the alliance with Poland would have precedence over any obligation to Prague.

---

[1]*German Documents*, II. 936. This minute was initialed by Weizsäcker, who forwarded it to Ribbentrop.

7.

**Conversations of the Polish Ambassador Józef Lipski
at Nuremberg, September 7-12, 1938**[1]

Strictly Confidential

(Excerpts)

---

[1]*Lipski Papers*, pp. 393-97, excerpts. Lipski was at Nuremberg with other members of the diplomatic corps to attend the annual convention of the National Socialist Party. This provided him with an opportunity for conversations with high German officials.

I. With Field Marshal Göring on September 9, 1938

(. . .)

(4) **Czechoslovakia.** Göring declared that the Karlsbad points request, among other things, dissolution by Czechoslovakia of the pact with Russia. Göring does not believe in the possibility of an agreement with Czechoslovakia. If the Czech government were to make an agreement, it would do so with the intention of breaking it. Even if Beneš were to accept its conditions, military elements would come out against it. From Göring's words it was clear that he is convinced that the necessity will arise to act by force. Göring shared the Ambassador's opinion that international armed conflict should be avoided. Göring thinks the problem should be placed on the League's agenda in order to define the aggressor. The Germans, though not members of the League, will be able to prove that they were not the aggressors. Before a decision is taken by the League, action in the field might already be finished. In Göring's opinion, France is simply looking for an honorable way out. England also is not willing to go to war and is exerting really strong pressure on Prague.

(. . .)

(6) **Rumania.** The Ambassador raised the question of the Havas Agency communiqué about the alleged Rumanian-Soviet agreement for Russian transit through Rumania. He pointed to the *démenti* issued by Bucharest. Göring questioned in detail the internal Rumanian situation, the King's role, his internal political plans, and, finally, the position of the new Rumanian envoy in Berlin, Djuvara.

(7) **Russia.** Göring stressed that in the future the real Russian attack against Germany could not be directed through Rumania or the Baltic states but only via Poland. Göring remarked that in case of a Polish-Russian conflict the Reich would come to Poland's assistance. A discussion followed about the situation in Russia and the strength of Russian armed forces.

(8) **Hungary.** Göring revealed a number of confidential bits of information from his conversations with Horthy (the first point, not mentioned here, was told to the Ambassador for his information under a word-of-honor plea for secrecy). Göring declared quite openly to the Hungarian side that under no circumstances would Germany act as intermediary in matters of interest to Hungary and Poland. The Hungarian government should settle these matters directly with Warsaw. Göring acted in this way in order to deprive Budapest of any illusion in this respect. Göring also pointed out to Horthy the necessity of granting broad autonomy to Slovakia. He did this in consequence of his last conversation with the Ambassador. Horthy was not too eloquent on this

point. Göring was under the impression that, in spite of Hungarian statements that in case Czechoslovakia were attacked by another state no Hungarian government could maintain itself in power unless it decided to act, Hungary would probably go into action very late.

(9) Horthy allegedly told the Chancellor that it would take England ten years to forgive Hungary if it attacked Czechoslovakia today. Hitler, upset by such a naive concept, replied that if this action took place in five years, when England would be armed to the teeth, it would be even less ready to forgive. Göring confirmed that territorial matters between Hungary and Poland are of no concern to Germany. The Germans are not prepared to pull chestnuts out of the fire for the Hungarians.

(. . .)

III. With Minister Ribbentrop on September 10, 1938

(. . .)

(3) **Czechoslovakia.** Ribbentrop: We strive for a solution by agreement. Beneš, as yet, has not granted any adequate concession. Misgivings as to Beneš' frankness. Remark that the Chancellor would never allow the provocation of May 21 to recur again. In such circumstances the Chancellor would definitely act by force, ignoring international repercussions, since then Germany's honor would be at stake.

Ribbentrop called attention to the anomaly of the signing of the Franco-Czech agreement at a moment when Germany was weak. The agreement was to serve the Czechs as an instrument to exert pressure on the Germans. In Ribbentrop's opinion, Great Britain would not budge on the Sudetenland case. France would encounter unyielding resistance with regard to armed intervention. Germany is now stronger than ever. The Ambassador declared it to be most important that the problem be solved locally to avoid international conflict. Ribbentrop replied that evidently no government would lightheartedly jump into an international brawl. Ribbentrop questioned our position on the Czechoslovak problem. The Ambassador replied that we are interested in a certain region. He stressed the necessity of autonomy for Slovakia. He pointed to the pro-Russian policy permanently pursued by Czechoslovakia, displayed in the geographical composition of the Czechoslovak state at the Peace Conference. In the course of further deliberations on this issue, when the Hungarian question was raised the conversation had to be interrupted.

(. . .)

Józef Lipski

90

Letter of Regent Miklós Horthy to Adolf Hitler Concerning the Settlement of the Czechoslovak Problem[1]

(no date)

Herr Führer and Chancellor of the Reich,

According to news reported mainly in the British press during the last few days there is an intention solving the Czechoslovak question in a way that the regions of Czechoslovakia inhabited by a German population would be separated with or without a plebiscite and transferred to the German Reich. In all other respects everything would remain as it is.

I believe it is unnecessary to point out that a settlement of this sort would fall short of a final solution of the Czech problem. This settlement could be imagined only in a way that all minorities settled in Czechoslovakian territory would be granted equal rights, i.e. that all nationalities of Czechoslovakia would be accorded the right to decide by way of a plebiscite on the sovereignty of the territories inhabited by them. Obviously, neither the Hungarian minority in Czechoslovakia, nor the Hungarian government could agree to a discrimination detrimental to our compatriots, and for this there is certainly full understanding on the part of the German government.

We are convinced that our opinion in this respect is in full harmony with that of the German Government, viz. that peace in Central Europe cannot be assured unless the Czechoslovak problem has been resolved definitively and radically.

In view of the extreme urgency of the Czechoslovak question, I have considered it necessary to call the attention of Your Excellency to this circumstance in the firm hope that as a token of the warm and friendly relations between our countries, I may reckon with the full support of Your Excellency in this grave hour.

Please accept, Your Excellency, the expression of my particular esteem.

(Typed draft in German, unsigned.)

---

[1]Horthy, Miklós, nagybányai. *The Confidential Papers of Admiral Horthy* (Miklós Szinay and László Szücs, compilers). Budapest: Corvina Press, 1965, pp. 101-102. The compilers refer to this as "a letter on a joint action against Czechoslovakia," even though the text makes no reference to action planned. The date of the posting of the letter has been tentatively established as September 17, 1938.

1863/423027-28

The Hungarian Legation in Germany
to the German Foreign Ministry[1]

MEMORANDUM

Berlin, September 28, 1938

(Pol. IV 6811)

Stoyadinovich expressed to Kánya his fear that, in the light of his information, the Hungarian Government had designs on the Slovak and Ruthenian areas besides the purely Hungarian areas. At the same time he stated that:

(1) if the Hungarian Government would give a satisfactory declaration regarding the security of Yugoslavia,

(2) if Hungary would state which areas of Slovakia we claim, he would be prepared, provided our claims did not extend to Slovak and Ruthenian areas, to attempt mediation in Prague, so that Prague should return to Hungary the Hungarian-inhabited areas.

From this it can be seen that Stoyadinovich would be ready to accept, or that he is reconciled to, the reassimilation of the Hungarian areas, but does not want a further strengthening of Hungary. He is apparently afraid that if the Ruthenes and Slovaks declared in favor of Hungary, and Hungary were thus strengthened, this might eventually become dangerous for Yugoslavia.

M. Kánya would be grateful if, in the interest of Hungary, Germany could, without mentioning the above information, but in the course of normal conversations, state in Belgrade that the Hungarian point of view, which aims at:

(a) the return of the Hungarian-inhabited areas,

(b) the practical realization of the right of self-determination for the Ruthenians and Slovaks, did not imply an aggressive attitude toward Yugoslavia, and that, in view of present-day circumstances, this would be the only correct solution.

---

[1]*German Documents*, II. 992. The document bears the comment (in Weizsäcker's handwriting): "Handed to me today by the Hungarian Minister," and instructions for the interested Missions to be circularized.

10.

Annex to the Munich Agreement[1]

His Majesty's Government in the United Kingdom and the French Government have entered into the above agreement on the basis that they stand by the offer, contained in paragraph 6 of the Anglo-French proposals of the 19th September, relating to an international guarantee of the new boundaries of the Czechoslovak State against unprovoked aggression.

When the question of the Polish and Hungarian minorities in Czecho-slovakia has been settled, Germany and Italy for their part will give a guarantee to Czechoslovakia.

Munich, September 29, 1938.

Adolf Hitler   *Edouard Daladier*
Neville Chamberlain   *Benito Mussolini*

---

[1]*International Legislation*, VIII. 134.

11.

Declaration Attached to the Munich Agreement[1]

The Heads of the Governments of the four Powers declare that the problems of the Polish and Hungarian minorities in Czechoslovakia, if not settled within three months by agreement between the respective Governments, shall form the subject of another meeting of the Heads of the Governments of the four Powers here present.

Munich, September 29, 1938.

Adolf Hitler   *Edouard Daladier*
Neville Chamberlain   *Benito Mussolini*

---

[1]*International Legislation*, VIII. 135.

12.

The Czechoslovak Minister (Hurban) to the Secretary of State[1]

760C.60F/287   Washington, October 1, 1938.

EXCELLENCY: I was instructed by my Government in a message received October first at 12:30 a.m. to communicate immediately to the Government of the United States the contents of Poland's ultimatum which was handed to the Czechoslovak Government shortly before midnight September thirtieth. My efforts to transmit the message during the night were unsuccessful.

Inasmuch as the Czechoslovak Government, according to later information, was forced to yield to the Polish demands, I have the honor to inform Your Excellency that the Czechoslovak Government considers the act of the Polish Government as a violation not only of the Briand-Kellogg Pact to which both States are signatories, but also of Paragraph 2 of the addenda to the agreement of the Four Powers reached at Munich on September 29th.

Accept. (etc.)

V. I. Hurban

---

[1]*U.S. Foreign Relations 1938*, I. 710.

13.

Telegraphic Circular of the Director
of the Political Department, German Foreign Ministry[1]

Berlin, October 1, 1938

zu Pol. IV 6621

Pol. IV 6811[2]

For Information.

According to information from Hungarian Minister here, the Yugoslav Prime Minister has informed Budapest that he would be willing to mediate in Prague about the cession to Hungary of areas of the former Czechoslovak State inhabited by Hungarians, if Hungary would issue a statement regarding security of Yugoslavia and would inform him what areas of Slovakia she claims. On the other hand, Yugoslavia would not agree to the cession to Hungary of strictly Slovak and Ruthenian territory, as this might be dangerous for Yugoslavia.

---

[1]*German Documents*, IV. 8. Addressed to the interested Missions.

[2]File numbers refer to documents reproduced *supra* as No. 6 and 9.

At the same time the Rumanian Government has also stated in Rome that it must reconsider its attitude in the event of Hungary's also putting forward claims to territory inhabited by a non-Hungarian population. For the rest, the Rumanian Minister in Rome has only emphasized that impulsive gestures on the part of Hungary cannot but render Rumania's international situation more difficult in view of her obligations arising out of the Little Entente.

The Hungarian Minister here has informed us that, apart from the re-integration of the region inhabited by Hungarians, Hungary in fact aims only at a realization of the right of self-determination of the Slovaks and Ruthenians, which has no kind of aggressive implication for Yugoslavia.

Postscript for all missions except Prague

Hungarian Minister has today announced Hungarian *démarche* in Prague in near future with a view to requesting the Prague Government to agree to immediate negotiations in the spirit of the Munich decisions. In accordance with his wishes very far-reaching German diplomatic support has in principle been promised to him. It was added that we could naturally only support demands of which we had an exact knowledge and must reserve the right to decide in individual cases.

Additional Postscript only for Budapest

Please follow a similar line in your capital.

For information: Prague Legation has been asked to put itself in contact with the Hungarian Minister there and to report by telegram upon the precise wording of Hungarian demands.

14.

140/76582-83

Circular of the State Secretary[1]

Telegram

Berlin, October 3, 1938

zu Pol. IV· 6891

The result achieved at the historic conference of the four leading statesmen of Europe at Munich, which did full justice to the demands put forward in the German memorandum, betokens an outstanding success for the policy of the Führer in general, as well as in the Sudeten-German question in particular. For the first time in history it has been possible to arrive by peaceful means at a frontier revision in the spirit of the peoples' right to self-determination.

---

[1]*German Documents*, IV. 18-19.

Fears expressed in the press of various countries of southeastern Europe that the outcome of Munich represents an act of dictation and simply means the first step toward further German territorial demands in southeastern Europe are completely groundless.

The Munich agreements amount to nothing more than the carrying into effect of the measures for the cession of Sudeten-German territory already conceded in principle by Czechoslovakia.

If, as in this case, the four leading Great Powers of Europe find themselves in complete agreement upon a European question, that can surely not just be overlooked in the future by the other European powers. But neither by the German Government, nor by the other powers concerned, as far as is known, are any plans or designs entertained of pursuing a joint policy of intervention.

(. . .)

Weizsäcker

15.

Mr. Newton (Prague) to Viscount Halifax[1]

Prague, October 3, 1938, 9.0 p.m.

Your telegram No. 408

During conversation with Minister for Foreign Affairs today I spoke to him on lines indicated. He explained that it was very difficult politically and even constitutionally to promise in advance in writing to cede Czechoslovakian territory. Verbally, however, he had made it quite clear to Hungarian Minister that such was definite and early intention of Czechoslovak Government and he thought Hungarian Government were satisfied.

Dr. Krofta made a somewhat pathetic appeal not to be forced to settle so important a matter absolutely immediately when he and the Government and their officials were already overwhelmed and worked to death with (Sudeten)[2] and Polish questions. He had suggested to Hungarian Minister that joint Commission should be set up in eight or ten days and it would be extremely difficult to find the Czechoslovak representatives for it before October 15. He would be grateful if His Majesty's Government would use their influence in this sense at Budapest. Dr. Krofta's verbal assurances are confirmed by a semi-official review of the position in Press today which ends by saying that in the circumstances explained Czechoslovak Government could not reject Hungarian claims for treatment similar to that of Germany and Poland.

---

[1]*British Documents*, III. 81-82.

[2]The text is here uncertain.

Additional reason for a few days delay is that discussion on mutual relations generally are proceding with Slovak representatives whose participation is desirable in negotiations with Hungary.

Repeated to Budapest, Paris, Rome and Berlin.

16.

140/75681

The German Chargé d'Affaires in Czechoslovakia
to the Foreign Ministry[1]

Telegram

No. 556 of October 4   Prague, October 4, 1938

11:05 p.m.
Received October 5
3:30 a.m.

According to reports here, independence movement in Slovakia is gaining ground steadily. Far-reaching autonomy is now demanded by political circles in Slovakia formerly loyal to Prague. A tendency is evident toward declaration of complete independence. According to press reports Černák, the newly appointed Slovak Minister, today handed his resignation to the President and told journalists that conditions in Slovakia were steadily deteriorating. Slovakia was being overrun by the Czechs.

Prague Government is endeavoring to reach agreement with Slovakia as soon as possible and at any price. Deputy Foreign Minister today spoke to me optimistically about probable outcome of negotiations at present in progress between Government and Slovak parties.

Hungarian Minister here stated that Budapest would regard voluntary union of Slovakia, including Carpatho-Ukraine,[2] with Hungary as the most practical solution of the Slovak question. In his personal view Slovakia could be given territorial autonomy *(Territorial Autonomie.)* Carpatho-Ukraine on the other hand, in view of the large Hungarian element of the population, could only be granted national autonomy *(National Autonomie.)* This would also be in accordance with Poland's wishes, as Warsaw feared a strengthening of Ukrainian nationalism as a result of territorial autonomy.

Polish Legation in Prague is more inclined to the idea on an independent Slovak State which would leave open the possibility of a protectorate under Poland or Hungary.

Hencke

---

[1] *German Documents,* IV. 32.

[2] Ruthenia.

140/76588

The German Chargé d'Affaires in Czechoslovakia to the Foreign Ministry[1]

No. 564 of October 5   Telegram   Prague, October 5, 1938
9:00 p.m.
Received October 6
1:00 p.m.

With reference to my telegram No. 555 of October 4.[2]

(1) Hungarian Minister today handed a note to the New Foreign Minister in which surprise is expressed that the answer to the Hungarian note[3] of October 3, promised for October 4, had not yet been received. In today's note the Hungarian Government demands an answer from Czechoslovakia and further makes an energetic protest against treatment and persecution of Hungarians in Czechoslovakia whereby good Czechoslovak-Hungarian relations would be endangered and prejudiced for the future. By the very nature of things Hungary and Czechoslovakia are at present in a state of excitement and, being aware of the Munich decisions, await their application with extreme anxiety. These conditions make it imperative that the necessary awards should be implemented immediately.

(2) The head of the European section of the Foreign Ministry told a member of the Legation that point 1 of the immediate measures demanded by Hungary (cf. telegram no. 545 of October 3) had already been fulfilled by the Czechoslovak Government and that this had been confirmed by note. Point 2 could not be carried out at once as the interpretation of Hungarian nationality could not be established forthwith. The Hungarian Legation itself was not clear about the type of measures demanded in point 3. There can be no discussion on point 4 (symbolic cession of territory) while Hungarian detachments which penetrated at Rimavská Sobota are still on Czechoslovak soil. The reconstruction of the Government had rendered impossible a complete answer to the Hungarian note within the time requested. The Czechoslovak Government envisaged October 15 as the date for the opening of negotiations and hoped that Germany would exert a moderating influence on the Hungarian Government.

Hencke

---

[1]*German Documents*, IV. 36-37.

[2]Reporting to Berlin that the "Czechoslovak Government for its part wished to reach direct agreement with Hungary as soon as possible. For technical and personal reasons, however, it was not possible to negotiate simultaneously with Germany, Poland, and Hungary. The Czechoslovak Government would therefore propose to Budapest that the start of the negotiations be postponed for a few days."

[3]Reproduced here as No. 41.

760F.62 1838

Report by the U.S. Military Attaché in Germany (Smith)[1]

No. 16,169   October 5, 1938

. . . There is today a mental conflict between Hitler's wishes [to retain Italy's friendship while winning France and England's] and Germany's national interest [an understanding with England at all costs.]

This conflict is apparent on October 5th, not only in the Mediterranean, but more particularly and immediately in the Hungarian-Czechish question. This latter question is on the surface one thing and under the surface quite another. If the surface aspect were the true one, the Hungarian problem would be settled tomorrow and the areas of Czechoslovakia which contain a Hungarian majority would be handed over to Hungary immediately. Actually the issue at stake is not the Hungarian districts of Slovakia, but Slovakia as a whole. The Hungarian Government wants the whole of Slovakia and Czechish Ruthenia, but never says so openly. Hungary's secret demand for Slovakia is championed by Mussolini and backed silently by Poland.

England and France want Slovakia to remain with Prague, largely out of a sense of shame for their desertion of her cause in the Sudeten issue. What the Slovaks want is not clear, so confused is the strength, grouping and platforms of the various political parties in Slovakia. Probably the majority of Slovaks would like to remain with Prague, but with a much larger degree of autonomy than has been theirs up to the present. Nevertheless there are potent elements in Slovakia who want an autonomous Slovakia within a Hungarian framework.

What does Hitler want? This is the present mystery of the German foreign policy. It is noticeable that Hitler's support of the Hungarians has been much less vociferous and much more reserved than Mussolini's, though if the issue were purely the Hungarian minority area passing to Hungary, Hitler would undoubtedly be in the first line fighting alongside Mussolini. Why isn't he doing so? Why does there appear to be a real difference of viewpoint between Hitler and Mussolini on the Hungarian question? The answer is believed to be Slovakia. Hitler must wish that Slovakia remain with Prague for military-political reasons, if for no other. Also to hand over Pressburg and the rest of Slovakia to Budapest would violate National Socialist tenets, "Men of the same race belong in the same state."

It is a military, political and economic disadvantage for Germany to have Slovakia pass to Hungary and for the following reasons:

---

[1]*U.S. Foreign Relations 1938, I. 716-720.*

Poland and Hungary obtain thereby common frontiers. Italy's position in Central Europe becomes thereby also immensely strong, for Hungary's acquisition of Slovakia brings into being automatically the grouping Italy—Yugoslavia—Hungary—Poland. This grouping is a far more serious military barrier to Germany's Danubian expansion than Czechoslovakia ever was.

If on the other hand Slovakia remains with Prague, Berlin can dominate both and incidentally keep a protective shield of her own between Warsaw and Budapest.

That Hitler would prefer to keep the Czechs and Slovaks together appears certain. On the other hand it seems doubtful if he can do so, for, for him to oppose openly Rome, Warsaw, and Budapest together at the present juncture, is out of the question.

It is a curious fact that five days after the meeting of Munich, Hitler finds himself in accord with France and England on the livest European issue and opposed to his allies, Poland, Hungary, and Italy. This is not to say that Hitler will not yield to Mussolini, if he has to do so. Only that he will seek to conceal his opposition behind France and possibly urge Prague to grant at once autonomy to Slovakia as a means of warding off a worse fate.

Hitler's diplomatic position at the moment is not an enviable one. He will require all of his diplomatic skill to avoid the many pitfalls which today confront him and hold to Italy while winning England and France.

There are two further sidelights of the European crisis which deserve the closest attention today and tomorrow.

1st. Poland has enormously strengthened its political-military position in Central Europe by the acquisition of the Olsa-Teschen area. This area looks small on the map, and to the uninformed the Teschen dispute seems to have been thought to be a minor matter of minorities. Actually Teschen is to Central Europe what the Panama Canal is to the Americas.

Teschen has rich coal and important steel industry. These by themselves make Teschen a rich prize. Still more important, however, is it that Teschen is the communication center of all Eastern Europe. Through the town and over the Jablunka Pass to the south runs the great north-south artery of Central Europe from Budapest to Prague and Breslau. Through it also run the lines from Vienna to Warsaw and the line from Prague to Slovakia and Ruthenia.

Poland now sits squarely across the main east-west line of inner communication of Czechoslovakia. Only minor unimportant routes over Pressburg and the mountains connecting Prague with her eastern provinces remain in her possession. Poland is now in a position where she can speak aggressively on Danubian matters and influence definitely the fate of Slovakia.

2nd. The second sidelight in the crisis worthy of close attention is the inner political struggle in progress behind the scenes in Hungary, the portent and probable outcome of which is not clearly apparent in Berlin at this time.

It is believed that the Hungarian National Socialists are seeking to secure power, that large elements of the Army support them, and that the feeling is strong in Hungary that Horthy and Imrédy have been too weak and unaggressive in the crisis of the past weeks; and that now through weakness, Hungary runs the risk of losing the Hungarian districts of Czechoslovakia. It is furthermore understood in Berlin that the Hungarian Nazis, unlike the Horthy-Imrédy regime, do not want Slovakia. This viewpoint of the Hungarian Nazis suggests that Hitler would welcome a Hungarian revolution. Such an outcome would undoubtedly obviate a clash with Mussolini.

19.

Sir H. Kennard (Warsaw) to Viscount Halifax[1]

Warsaw, October 6, 1938, 4:45 p.m.

My immediately preceding telegram.

Polish Government would undoubtedly like to secure a common frontier with Hungary. Responsible members of the Ministry of Foreign Affairs favour attainment of this by grant of autonomy to Ruthenia under Hungarian suzerainty. They point out that there is a 20 per cent Hungarian minority there and that if Hungarian districts are detached including essential railways therein, the rest of Ruthenia cannot exist. Semi-official "Gazeta Polska" today states that in any case Czechoslovakia never had any proper historical or economic claim to Ruthenia which was a bridge-head for Czecho-Soviet cooperation. For centuries Poland and Hungary had a common frontier. The problem of Ruthenia's restitution to Hungary was a Polish problem and involved Poland's military security. Attitude now adopted by Czechoslovak Government towards Ruthenia would be of cardinal importance and would prove whether Prague intended to accept Poland's outstretched hand of friendship.

2. According to official Polish telegraph agency all parties in Ruthenia except Communists are agreed in demanding a plebiscite to decide future of territory.

---

[1]*British Documents*, III. 111-112.

3. I hear that the question of the future of Ruthenia is causing excitement in the Ukrainian districts of Poland.

4. The question of Slovakia's future status has become more acute since my interview with the Vice-Minister for Foreign Affairs on October 3 (see my telegram No. 75 Saving).

An evidently inspired article in the "Gazeta Polska" today says that the movement for independence is growing in Slovakia and that Poland would view with great satisfaction "any improvement in the national existence of the Slovaks." According to official Polish telegraph agency report from Bratislava this morning political circles there are pleased that "both Poland and Hungary adopted a favourable attitude to the Slovak independence and are ready to give guarantees to an independent Slovak State."

The Polish and Hungarian Governments are evidently in very close co-operation. The Hungarian Minister for Foreign Affairs' Chef de Cabinet flew here yesterday and is to see M. Beck today.

I understand that my Rumanian colleague saw M. Beck, having been instructed by his Government to make representations regarding the Polish attitude towards future of Ruthenia.

M. Beck told him that the Polish Government favoured the return of Ruthenia to Hungary.

He further said that it was expected that the Slovaks would declare their independence today and indicated that such a small Slav State would have to maintain closest relations with her northern neighbour.

Repeated to Prague, Paris, Berlin, Rome, Bucharest and Budapest.

20.

Viscount Halifax to Mr. Newton (Prague)[1]

FOREIGN OFFICE, October 6, 1938

9:30 p.m.

Your telegram No. 861

The Hungarian Minister saw Sir A. Cadogan on October 3 and asked that His Majesty's Government would use their friendly influence in Prague in order to promote the success of the negotiations regarding the Hungarian claim which had, he said, already been initiated.

Sir A. Cadogan did not promise that we should take this action, but I nevertheless think it would be useful if you were to inform the Minister for Foreign Affairs of the instructions sent to Sir G. Knox in my telegram[2] No. 96 and were on the strength of these to urge upon the Minister for

---

[1]*British Documents*, III. 113-114.

[2]Reproduced here as No. 21.

Foreign Affairs if you see no objection the importance of initiating conversations with the Hungarian Government without delay and of bringing them to a conclusion as soon as possible.

Rumanian Minister, who is much alarmed at Polish and Hungarian activities regarding Slovakia and Ruthenia, suggests that the continual pressure of these two countries will force the Czechs, now that they are deserted by the Western Powers, to turn more and more to Germany in the hope that latter will in her own interest oppose further cession of territory by Czechoslovakia. Do you support this view or have you any reason to expect that, as a result of Dr. Beneš' resignation or for other reasons, we may now expect a reorientation of Czechoslovak foreign policy?

Repeated to Budapest, Paris, Warsaw, Bucharest, Berlin and Rome.

21.

Viscount Halifax to Sir G. Knox (Budapest)[1]

FOREIGN OFFICE, October 6, 1938

10.0 p.m.

Prague telegrams Nos. 861[2] and 867.

Similar appeal was made October 4 by Czechoslovak Minister here in memorandum of which following are chief points:

(1) Czechoslovak Government fully appreciate urgent need for "stable and working arrangement" with Hungary involving transfer of territory, but think it imperative that this should not be done under pressure from Hungary.

(2) They do not intend to procrastinate, but preoccupation with German and Polish claims makes it technically impossible for them to settle at once with Hungary.

(3) Great Britain, France and Italy should induce Hungary to negotiate peacefully: otherwise armed conflict might ensue, involving Rumania and Yugoslavia as well. These Powers should employ same tactics at Budapest as they employed at Prague in regard to German demands.

(4) Czechoslovak Government could open diplomatic negotiations with Hungarian Government in ten days or fortnight (from October 4) and diplomatic discussions even sooner—but only if there is no ultimatum.

(5) Czechoslovak Government assure His Majesty's Government that their desire for agreement is "sincere and unflinching." They authorise His Majesty's Government to inform the Hungarian Government of this assurance.

[1] British Documents, III. 115-116.
[2] Reproduced here as No. 15.

Please bring points (1), (2), (4) and (5) above to the knowledge of the Hungarian Minister for Foreign Affairs and, after expressing appreciation of the manner in which the Hungarians have hitherto put forward their claims against Czechoslovakia, express to him the hope that they will in future refrain from making demands in such a manner or of such a nature as to prejudice the prospects of that peaceful agreement which the Czechoslovak Government have announced their anxiety to reach. You should then communicate to Minister for Foreign Affairs the text of Sir T. Inskip's statement about the British guarantee.[1] You might add an expression of hope that the Hungarian press will do nothing to aggravate situation (see Bucharest telegram No. 233 to Foreign Office).

You should then mention that the Hungarian Minister on October 3 asked us to use our influence at Prague to induce the Czechoslovak Government to enter into negotiations and to conclude an agreement with the Hungarians with the least possible delay and should inform Minister for Foreign Affairs of the instructions sent to Mr. Newton in my telegram No. 438.[2]

I understand that your French colleague will be receiving instructions to make similar representations in this sense.

Repeated to Warsaw, Prague, Paris, Berlin, Bucharest and Rome.

---

[1] The reference is to Sir T. Inskip's statement in the House of Commons on October 4 in answer to a question whether the British guarantee to Czechoslovakia was already in operation. Sir T. Inskip, Minister for the Coordination of Defence, said that the formal treaty of guarantee had not yet been drawn up, and that therefore technically the guarantee could not be said to be in force. He added: "His Majesty's Government, however, feel under a moral obligation to Czechoslovakia to treat the guarantee as being now in force. In the event, therefore, of an act of unprovoked aggression against Czechoslovakia, His Majesty's Government would certainly feel bound to take all steps in their power to see that the integrity of Czechoslovakia is preserved." *Parl. Deb.*, 5th Ser., H. of C., Vol. 339, cols. 295-308.

[2] Reproduced here as Document 20.

383/210819

22.

The Supreme Command of the Wehrmacht
to the Foreign Ministry[1]

Secret

Berlin, October 6, 1938

Pol. I.M. 3855 g.

No. 0168/38 geh. Ausl. Ic. 2 Ang.

Reference: No. 0168/geh. usl. Ic. of Oct. 5, 1938

Subject: Establishment of a common frontier between Poland and Hungary

[1] *German Documents*, IV. 40.

The creation of a compact bloc of succession states on Germany's eastern frontier, with lines of communication to southeast Europe, will not be to our interest. Accordingly, a statement to that effect was addressed to the Foreign Ministry by the Supreme Command of the Wehrmacht on October 5, 1938, saying "that *for military reasons* a common Hungarian-Polish frontier was undesirable."

It is assumed that in the future the "Czech and Slovak" Rump State will of necessity depend to a considerable extent on Germany. The conditions for this are now present, especially as in Czechoslovakia strong feeling prevails against Britain and France, by whom she feels betrayed. Moreover a strong tendency is developing toward dissolving the relationship of the Czechs to the U.S.S.R. at the earliest possible moment.

Consequently, it is in our *military interest* that Slovakia should not be separated from the Czechoslovak union but should remain with Czechoslovakia under strong German influence.

By order of the Chief of Staff of the Supreme Command of the Wehrmacht.

(Signature)

23.

383/210762-68

Memorandum by the Director of the Political Department[1]

Berlin, October 7, 1938

I submit a memorandum for the Führer on the Slovak and Carpatho-Ukraine question.

To the Foreign Minister.

Woermann

(Enclosure)

MEMORANDUM FOR THE FÜHRER

In view of the negotiations due to begin in the next few days between Hungary and Czechoslovakia, it is necessary to define our policy on the Slovak and Carpatho-Ukraine question.

I

Slovak Question

Four possibilities in theory:

1. Independent Slovakia
2. Slovak autonomy within the Czechoslovak State

---

[1]*German Documents*, IV. 46-49.

3. Autonomous Slovakia oriented toward Hungary, which might develop from alliance into incorporation

4. Autonomous Slovakia oriented toward Poland.

Ref. 1) The question of the economic viability of a completely independent Slovakia is doubtful but could be answered in the affirmative if Germany provided support. Very rich in timber; part of the Czechoslovak armament industry lies in Slovak territory (Waag and Gran Valley). Geologically not yet fully explored, old inactive mining area, of which a part is again being worked. Possibilities for the future in this region. At all events favorable conditions for intensifying economic union with Germany. Common frontier will be set up.

An independent Slovakia would be weak constitutionally and would therefore best further the German need for penetration and settlement in the east. Point of least resistance in the east.

Ref. 2) Since the resolutions passed at Sillein on October 6 by all the Slovak parties and the subsequent agreement with the Czech Government, an autonomous Slovak Government has now been formed in conjunction with Czechia (Tschechei). According to reports so far received the State presidency, foreign policy, and finance are to be common to both, while Slovakia is to have an independent military organization. The relationship would be similar to that between the old Austria and Hungary. We could tolerate that solution for the present. It even presents certain advantages compared with an independent Slovakia. This presupposes that the future Czecho-Slovakia will have a strong leaning toward Germany in political and economic matters, and evidence of a readiness for this is now apparent. A complete separation between Czechia and Slovakia would always be possible later. The complete structure of Czecho-Slovakia be stronger than two independent structures. If we exercise decisive influence on Prague, Hungary's and Poland's chances of making Slovakia a permanent bone of contention would be lessened.

From the point of view of foreign policy the solution of a Slovakia united with Czechia is the easiest of achievement. After the Slovak leaders have declared in favor of this solution it could be recognized by us under the slogan of "self determination."

The decision lies therefore between solutions 1 and 2, while solution 1, i.e. an independent Slovakia, would still remain open for the future if the Czecho-Slovak solution is decided on for the present.

Ref. 3) Hungary is striving for some form of union of an autonomous Slovakia with Hungary. Germany has no interest in this solution. Slovaks themselves strongly reject any form of union with Hungary.

Ref. 4) Our interest in an autonomous Slovakia oriented toward Poland is even less than in one oriented toward Hungary. By her acqui-

106

sition of the Teschen district Poland has already considerably increased her power in this area. The addition of Slovakia to the Polish economic sphere might put considerable difficulties in the way of German economic aspirations toward the southeast.

II

Carpatho-Ukraine Question

An independent Carpatho-Ukrainian State without support from outside at present is hardly viable. The advantage of this solution, however, would be that a nucleus for a greater Ukraine in the future would be created here. The many million Ukrainians in Poland, the Soviet Union, and Rumania would be given a motherland and thus become national minorities.

In any case autonomy for the Carpatho-Ukraine under the slogan of self-determination should be demanded, and on this there are hardly any differences of opinion. Orientation of the autonomous Ukraine to Hungary is to be definitely rejected. This solution is desired by Hungary as well as Poland. A common Polish-Hungarian frontier would thereby be created, which would facilitate the formation of an anti-German bloc. From a military, point of view the Supreme Command of the Wehrmacht is also opposed to this common Polish-Hungarian frontier.

While rejecting the Hungarian solution and assuming that an independent Carpatho-Ukraine is not viable, the remaining solution would be an autonomous Carpatho-Ukraine oriented to Slovakia or Czechoslovakia. This is the most natural solution for the present. It leaves other possibilities open for a later date, and it can also be achieved under the slogan "self-determination." Regarding the demarcation of the Carpatho-Ukraine from Slovakia there are questions of detail which have still to be examined.

III

German Language Enclaves

With the exception of Pressburg, there are no German-language enclaves in the area, immediate cession of which is claimed by Hungary. Most important groups: Proben and Kremnitz language enclave with about 50,000 Germans, Upper and Lower Zips about 40,000; less important new settlements in the Ukrainian area north of Munkatsch about 15,000 Germans. There should be no transfer of population from these language enclaves, as they are of value as a nucleus for further development in the east. Transfer from the Kremnitz area is possible for some of those who already are coming to Germany for seasonal work.

107

Summary

1. For Slovakia: Alternatives—independent Slovakia or Czechoslovak solution. Both presuppose orientation toward Germany. For the outside world, a slogan of "right of self-determination," which leaves open the possibility of a plebiscite in Slovakia.

2. For Carpatho-Ukraine: Alternatives—support for an independent but scarcely viable Carpatho-Ukraine and orientation toward Slovakia or Czechoslovakia. For the outside world the slogan also to be "right of self-determination" with the possibility of a plebiscite when the time comes.

3. From this results a rejection of the Hungarian or Polish solution for Slovakia as well as for Carpatho-Ukraine. In rejecting the demands of both those powers we would have a good slogan in the phrase "self-determination." For the outside world no anti-Hungarian or anti-Polish slogans are to be issued.

4. Steps can be taken to influence leading persons in Slovakia and Carpatho-Ukraine in favor of our solution. Preparations for this are already on foot.

24.

Letter of Regent Miklós Horthy to British Prime Minister Neville Chamberlain Asking for the Support of Hungarian Territorial Claims[1]

October 8, 1938

Dear Mr. Chamberlain:

It is not in my official capacity as the Regent of Hungary that I am writing this letter to you, but as Admiral Horthy, a simple Hungarian, who loves his country above all. Three years ago I had the pleasure of meeting your brother, Sir Austin, as my guest here. He showed great interest in all the questions concerning my country—the wrongs and injustices done to her. Sir Austin understood that Hungary's claims are just and fair, and told me when I asked him to give me his advice: "Keep quiet now, I promise you, when the right moment comes, England will help you."—The past years prove that I carried out loyally his advice—I kept quiet and waited for the right moment to come!

But I think I am justified in saying: the right moment has come. Therefore I am now appealing to you—the man who has shown so much generosity, wisdom, and courage, asking you to accept as your legacy, your late brother's promise to me to help us, and do all in your own and your great country's power to assist and help us in this eventful hour.

I pledge my word that you will never have to regret it, and assure you of the undying gratitude of the entire Hungarian nation.

(Typed, unsigned copy in English)

---

[1] Horthy, *Confidential Papers*, pp. 104-105.

25.

1648/391407-10

Unsigned Memorandum[1]

Telephone Message

Godesberg, October 12, 1938

4:45 p.m.

For the State Secretary.

In his conversation with the Foreign Minister at Godesberg on October 11, the Führer made the following decisions:

(. . .)

IX

As for the question of Pressburg, complete reserve is at first to be exercised in principle, and all questions connected with this problem are to be subjected to the most careful examination. Should the Hungarians approach us with demands for Pressburg, the following statement is to be made to them:

(a) In principle Germany sympathizes with Hungarian demands on Czechoslovakia.

(b) The Führer has repeatedly said that Germany can only draw the sword for German interests.

(c) The Führer invited the Hungarian Prime Minister and Foreign Minister to visit him at Obersalzberg and there advised them both to press their cause somewhat more energetically. In the critical days which followed, the Hungarians did nothing and this explains their present difficult diplomatic situation.

(d) If any points of difference remain, a plebiscite under international control must take place.

IX

For the personal information of the State Secretary.

Should Hungary mobilize, it is not our intention to hamper the Hungarians or even advise them to use moderation.

---

[1]*German Documents*, IV. 54-56.

26.

140/75826

The Minister in Hungary to the Foreign Ministry[1]

Telegram

No. 129 of October 13. Budapest, October 13, 1938—10:56 p.m.

Received October 14—3:20 a.m.

With reference to telephone message today to Under State Secretary Woermann.

Prime Minister informed me that his predecessor, Darányi, had been instructed to clear away certain misunderstandings which appeared to have arisen between Germany and Hungary and to clarify the views of both parties.

The attitude of the German press toward the creation of a common frontier between Poland and Hungary in Carpatho-Ukraine had caused astonishment here. The idea suggested in the French press of Hungarian participation in any formation of a Polish-Rumanian bloc against Germany was absurd as the Carpathians form a natural barrier only against the east. With the reincorporation of Carpatho-Ukraine, Hungary would prolong the Rumanian front against Bolshevism and form a strong bulwark against it on the Carpathian passes.

The events of recent months caused the Hungarian Government to feel itself bound more firmly than ever to the Berlin-Rome Axis and it was prepared to affirm this on paper. The question of the Pressburg bridgehead is not to be raised by Darányi.

Erdmannsdorf

[1]*German Documents, IV. 66.*

27.

140/75801

The Minister in Hungary to the Foreign Ministry[1]

Telegram

Urgent Budapest, October 13, 1938—10:56 p.m.

No. 132 of October 13 Received October 14-1:40 a.m.

Prime Minister informed me that if the Czechoslovaks, whose counterproposal of this morning was completely unsatisfactory, did not change their attitude, the Hungarian Government would order mobiliza-

[1]*German Documents. IV, 67.*

tion within 24 hours, presumably without making its intermediate demand announced in yesterday's telegraphic report.[2] This would result in the doubling of the present strength of the army. This measure did not mean war but was necessary because Czech demobilization had not yet taken place. Hungary was ready to march if we gave our consent. Unrest in the Hungarian area of Czechoslovakia was constantly increasing.

The Foreign Minister's Chief de Cabinet has just stated that negotiations in Komárom had been broken off. The Hungarian Government will appeal to the four Great Powers and inform them of the course of the negotiations.

Erdmannsdorf

---

[2]The telegram reported that the Hungarians intended first to demand that the Czechs demobilize on their frontier by a certain date; in the absence of a favorable reply, they would themselves mobilize.

28.

Draft Declaration Signed by Regent Miklós Horthy on the Interruption of the Czechoslovak-Hungarian Negotiations[1]

October 13, 1938

The resolution passed in the four-power conference in Munich on September 29th decreed that if the problem of Polish and Hungarian minorities could not be settled by an agreement of the governments interested within three months, this would devolve upon another conference of the chiefs of the governments present in Munich. Obviously the conference had in mind a solution by which the territories inhabited by Poles and Hungarians would be handed over to Poland and Hungary, respectively. This was the underlying principle of the negotiations to be started between the two countries.

No sooner was Hungary advised of the resolutions than its government immediately applied to the Czechoslovak government proposing to take up negotiations without delay, and on October 3rd, forwarded a note suggesting that the negotiations be opened on October 6th. Simultaneously, a few appropriate demands were put forward to guarantee that negotiations would be continued in earnest. In response to this action the Czechoslovak government in principle replied in the affirmative, yet actually it used delaying tactics, until finally on October 9th the negotiations were opened.

Before negotiations started, the Czechoslovak government on several occasions had expressed to the Hungarian representative, and then also publicly, through broadcasts, the press, etc., that they do not want

---

[1]Horthy, *Confidential Papers*, pp. 105-107.

national minorities to remain within their frontiers in the course of the reconstruction of their country, but would be prepared to cede these minorities and the territories inhabited by them.

This meant that there was agreement on principle between the great powers, Czechoslovakia and Hungary. This agreement in principle could be construed in no other way than the territories inhabited by a Magyar majority would be ceded to Hungary. At determining these territories, obviously the start would have to be made from the further principle, which had been applied to the Sudeten country, that the conditions of twenty years before, i.e. the data of the latest census before that date could be accepted as a basis. This thesis holds to an even greater extent as regards the Hungarians, the question involving a territory which before was part of Hungary, yet, as has been explicitly shown by the Munich resolutions, was detached from her wrongfully by denying the Wilsonian principles. Obviously, at the settlement the changes that have occurred in the composition of the population, being based on unlawfulness and injustice, cannot be taken into consideration, and consequently the conditions before the commitment of unlawfulness and injustice have to be reverted to.

Despite this, in the opening negotiations on October 9th, the Czechoslovak government adopted an attitude on the ceding of these territories, which cannot be justified, and which shows that the Czechoslovak government want to evade the assertion of the principle of cessation of territories, and betrays their intention to hold dominion over foreign nationalities against the latter's will.

The Czechoslovak government rely for this point of view exclusively on considerations of power, and in order to assert these considerations do not carry out the demobilization of the army as decided nominally, but using this mobilized army want to exert pressure on Hungary which has not mobilized.

The Hungarian government have done their utmost to carry through the settlement laid down in the Munich agreement by the most peaceful means, by way of negotiations continued in a friendly spirit. However, the Hungarian government feel compelled to state that neither the spirit in which negotiations have been opened, not the Czechoslovak proposals put forward during the negotiations, nor the circumstance of maintaining the army in a mobilized state with the hope of influencing the progress of the negotiations are attitudes to be tolerated any longer without strong objections. Furthermore there is every indication that these attitudes are purposeful evasions of rightful Hungarian claims.

For this very reason the Hungarian government have decided to interrupt the negotiations, and without delay inform the four parties to the Munich agreement of the actual state of negotiations, (and in order

112

to ensure further negotiations being continued on an equal footing
decree the general mobilization of the army.)[2]

Horthy

---

[2]The last passage in this typed draft, signed by Horthy, was crossed out by him in pencil.
There was no general mobilization, instead, on October 17th, five age groups were called
to arms. There is no proof that the declaration was ever published, and it fell on the
Minister of Foreign Affairs to inform the interested powers. (See below, Hungarian communication to Berlin, London, Paris, Rome and Warsaw, October 14, 1938.)

29.

Letter of Regent Miklós Horthy to Adolf Hitler on the Interruption of the Czechoslovak-Hungarian Negotiations[1]

October 13, 1938

Your Excellency:

The negotiations with the Czechoslovak Republic had to be interrupted tonight. The counter-proposals of the Czechoslovak government
were wholly unacceptable, inasmuch as these proposals included only a
fraction of the territory inhabited by a Hungarian majority, and in addition, apart from the town of Komárom situated on the Danube, not a
single one of the many Hungarian towns was included in them. These
proposals were put forward after negotiations had been protracted for
several days, and in addition accompanied by menacing statements over
the radio which for our part we could not accept without a reply. Besides,
our co-nationals living in the occupied territory are harassed, their food-
stuffs and cattle are taken from them with force. For this reason I should
like to inform Your Excellency without delay that in all likelihood I shall
be forced to decree the mobilization of the army the more so since
Czechoslovakia is still in a mobilized state.

Simultaneously, I would request Your Excellency to grant us an
opportunity for a thorough and urgent discussion to make clear certain
questions which are partly independent of it. I should be very grateful if
Your Excellency had time to receive if possible tomorrow the former
Prime Minister Darányi, who carries my instructions as representative of
the government. He is ready to leave by airplane immediately . . .

(Unsigned, typed draft in German)

---

[1]Horthy, *Confidential Papers*, pp. 107-108. A similar letter was sent to Mussolini, and
subsequently Count Csáky was dispatched to Rome for an "urgent discussion."

Final Declaration of the Hungarian Delegation in Komárom[1]

Ainsi que nous avons eu l'honneur de déclarer à plusieurs reprises, nous sommes venus ici animés des meilleures intentions et dans la plus sincère espoir qu'il nous sera possible d'arriver rapidement à un accord qui donnera des bases solides aux relations entre nos Etats.

A notre plus vif regret, cet espoir ne s'est pas réalisé.

Je ne voudrais pas, à cette occasion, me référer à nouveau à certains symptômes défavorables, car nous l'avons fait plusieurs fois au cours des négociations.

Je dois cependant constater et souligner que la contre-proposition tchécoslovaque concernant les nouvelles frontières qui nous a été remise ce matin est tellement différente de notre conception et que concernant les bases du nouveau réglement les thèses représentées par les deux Délégations sont séparées d'un abîme sur lequel, selon notre conviction, il est impossible de jeter un pont par les présentes négociations.

Pour ces motifs, le Gouvernement Royal de Hongrie a décidé de considérer ces négociations, en ce qui le concerne, comme terminées et de demander le réglement urgent de ses revendications territoriales vis-à-vis la Tchécoslovaquie, des quatre grandes puissances signataires du Protocole de Munich.

---

[1]Ádám, A müncheni egyezmény . . . , p. 772. The declaration was read by Foreign Minister Kánya in Hungarian, and handed to the Czechoslovak delegation in French.

30.

140/75824

The Minister in Hungary to the Foreign Ministry[1]

Telegram

Immediate   Budapest, October 14, 1938—5:25 a.m.

No. 133 of October 14   Received October 14—9:15 a.m.

Count Csáky informed me at 3 a.m. that the Council of Ministers had just passed a resolution to call up five more classes by individual orders but to refrain from making a public announcement of this partial mobilization until the attitude of the German and Italian Governments was known.

Ex-Prime Minister Darányi is flying to Munich at 9 a.m. today and Count Csáky to Rome in order to ascertain this.

Erdmannsdorf

---

[1]*German Documents*, IV. 67-68.

31.

Mr. Newton (Prague) to Viscount Halifax[1]

Prague, October 15, 1938, 2:15 a.m.

My telegrams Nos. 959 and 962.

I was received this evening by Dr. Krno, Political Director at Ministry of Foreign Affairs, who had returned this morning from Komárno.

He left with me statement of Czechoslovak case of which following is a translation:

"Czechoslovak delegation had gome to Komárno with firm desire to reach lasting, fair, and rapid settlement.

(1) They had agreed to open negotiations not later than ten days after Munich Agreement though it had contemplated a delay of three months;

(2) To show their readiness to make territorial sacrifices they had agreed on first day of negotiations to symbolic cession of Sahý and station of Nové Mesto;

(3) They had proposed a frontier involving cession of about 400,000 persons including 330,000 Hungarians and leaving approximately the same number of Hungarians in Czechoslovakia as Slovaks and Ruthenes in Hungary;

(4) They had emphasized that even this proposal was not final and that they wished to continue discussions on basis of mutual concessions.

The attitude of the Hungarian delegation had on the other hand been as follows:

(1) They had submitted proposal, which would not only have deprived Slovakia of nearly all her important towns and vital lines of communication but have involved cession of about 510,000 Slovaks and Ruthenes (apart from 300,000 already in Hungary) leaving only about 20,000 Hungarians in Czechoslovakia;

(2) They had refused to put forward second proposal despite earnest request of Czechoslovak delegation;

(3) They had abruptly broken off negotiations only a few days after their opening."

In further conversation Dr. Krno emphasized that figures which Hungarian delegation had produced were entirely different from Czech figures based on the same 1910 census. He added that Austrians had had similar experience of unreliability of Hungarian figures in dispute over Burgenland. Good commentary on Hungarian figures was fact that

---

[1]*British Documents*, III. 184-186.

Dr. Tiso, head of Czechoslovak delegation appeared . . .[2] as a Hungarian.

Dr. Krno made further point that Hungarians had demanded amongst other things plebiscite for Slovaks and Ruthenes, a matter which was no concern of theirs.

His personal feeling was that Hungarians had received encouragement from Italy.

Somewhat surprisingly he did not in speaking to me challenge the main principle of Hungarian argument that 1910 census should be used as basis. Its acceptance by the Powers would nevertheless ripen by international agreement the points [sic ?fruits], subsequently surrendered, of 50 years of a Magyarisation policy which has been generally condemned (see Macartney's "Hungary and her Neighbours", page 2).

Repeated to Berlin, Budapest, Rome, Warsaw, Bucharest and Belgrade.

---

[2]A word appears to have been omitted here.

32.

Conversation of the Polish Ambassador Józef Lipski with Reich Minister of Foreign Affairs von Ribbentrop at Berchtesgaden on October 24, 1938[1]

(Excerpts)

Polish Embassy in Berlin
Strictly Confidential

(. . .)

II. Hungary's Revindications

Herr von Ribbentrop exposed at length his personal objections to the Hungarian way of behavior. He recalled that during Horthy's visit the Chancellor quite frankly told the Regent that he had decided to act on the problem of the Sudetenland, and he advised the Hungarians to be ready for any eventuality. During this visit, to the utter surprise of the German government, Kánya showed Ribbentrop a communiqué from Bled,[2] which evidently made the worst possible impression in Berlin. The Hungarian side, during this visit, constantly warned against war entanglements, owing to the Anglo-French stand. It came to Ribbentrop's knowledge that upon their return to Budapest the rumor was spread there that he was conducting a madman's policy. Ribbentrop's resentment centered mainly on Kánya.

He further mentioned that on the eve of the Godesberg Conference the Chancellor invited Imrédy to Berchtesgaden and gave him detailed

---

[1]*Lipski Papers*, pp. 453-58.

[2]See Document No. 2, above.

information on the situation. On Imrédy's request, the Chancellor firmly supported Hungarian claims at the conference in Munich. Hungarians knew all about this, but not a single word of thanks followed, since they considered that German efforts were self-explanatory.

Next, von Ribbentrop discussed the Problem of the German government's mediation. In the conversations with Darányi at Berchtesgaden the Hungarian ethnographic line was discussed. It was established that Bratislava would remain outside the line and that Nitra would be subject to a plebiscite; Koszyce (Košice) would remain within the Hungarian line, while Užhorod and Munkacz (Mukačevo) would fall beyond the line (as far as I could understand, they were to be subject to a plebiscite).

Ribbentrop used his influence on Chvalkovský to accept such a Hungarian line and discussed it also with the Slovaks and representatives of Carpathian Ruthenia.

The Slovaks were hurt by the Koszyce question; the representative of Carpathian Ruthenia was rather pleased that Užhorod and Munkacz had been left outside the line of claims.

Ribbentrop emphasized here that he did not take any sides and was acting merely as a mediator.

When the results of these conversations were communicated to Budapest by Erdmannsdorf, the Hungarian government bluntly rejected the proposal, in spite of Darányi's earlier approval. Under these circumstances the German government withdrew from mediation and washed its hands of the matter. The Italian side, informed about this, is allegedly also discouraged to some extent by the Hungarian methods.

Ribbentrop is of the opinion that, as matters stand, talks will continue for the time being between Budapest and Prague.

Asked about arbitration, he replied that at present he does not think arbitration could take place; besides, he raises the following objections:

1) Whether, with two other signatories of the Munich Agreement, arbitration with the participation of Germany and Italy would be possible.

2) In case of arbitration, its execution should be guaranteed. Here a military engagement would possibly be needed.

For my part, in accordance with my instruction, I only stated that, in case Germany and Italy agree on arbitration, Poland would join it also.

In my discussion with Ribbentrop I laid special detailed emphasis on our stand regarding the Polish-Hungarian frontier and Carpathian Ruthenia. I am not repeating my arguments here. I think that Ribbentrop was impressed by the Ukrainian argument contained in your instructions. In conclusion he said he would still reconsider this matter in the light of my deliberations. He asked whether we had territorial claims to Ruthenia; I replied that we did not, that we limited ourselves to support of Hungarian claims to that country.

Ribbentrop pointed here to difficulties created by Rumania's attitude, stressing the Reich's desire to maintain good relations with that country. He was also informed that Rumania does not insist on a territorial revision in Carpathian Ruthenia to its advantage.

(. . .)

VI. Polish Matters

Ribbentrop stressed that in conversations with him the Chancellor kept returning to his idea of finding a solution to the Jewish problem through an organization for the purpose of emigration. We had an exhaustive talk on this subject. Ribbentrop interrogated me at length on the Jewish situation in Poland.

Speaking about our action with regard to Teschen,[3] Ribbentrop remarked that the Chancellor repeated again and again to the circle of his collaborators his appreciation for our determined move, stating: "The Poles are tough guys. Pilsudski would be proud of them."

Józef Lipski

---

[3]Immediately after the Munich Agreement, Poland presented an ultimatum to Prague and occupied the Teschen territory.

33.

Viscount Halifax to the Earl of Perth (Rome)[1]

No. 476 Telegraphic (C 12924-2319-12)

Foreign Office, October 26, 1938. 9:20 p.m.

Berlin telegram No. 632.1.

Czechoslovak Minister informed me this morning on instructions that his Government regarded as quite unacceptable the Hungarian demand for plebiscites in the disputed districts on the basis of the 1910 census. On the other hand, the Czechoslovak Government would be in favour of arbitration by Germany and Italy. In response to an enquiry, M. Masaryk later ascertained from Prague that his Government were opposed to Poland being included among the arbitrators and thought that if Poland were included, Rumania should be included also. M. Masaryk said that the Czechoslovak Government would have to reply today to the Hungarian demand, and before doing so wished to have the views of His Majesty's Government on their attitude.

In reply the Czechoslovak Minister was informed this afternoon that His Majesty's Government saw no objection to the settlement of the Czech-Hungarian question by means of arbitration by Germany and

---

[1]British standpoint of October 26, 1938, concerning the settlement of the Hungaro-Czechoslovak question by arbitration. *British Documents,* III. 202.

118

Italy, if the Czechoslovak and Hungarian Governments agree to settle their differences this way. It was added that if the two parties to the dispute preferred to refer the matter to the four Munich powers, His Majesty's Government would be ready to join in any discussions.

If the views of the Italian Ambassador, reported in Berlin telegram under reference, represent those of his Government, it seems that the Italian Government would prefer that Great Britain and France, as signatories of the Munich Agreement, should participate in any arbitration. If this is indeed the attitude of the Italian Government, it is no doubt occasioned by their desire to obtain support against Germany, who is believed to oppose the acquisition of Ruthenia by Hungary. Herr von Ribbentrop may of course settle the whole question when he arrives in Rome tomorrow, but it may be of value to the Italian Government to have an indication of our views on this question before the German Minister for Foreign Affairs arrives.

I should therefore be glad if you would seek an early interview with the Italian Minister for Foreign Affairs and inform him that while it is difficult for us to adjudicate between the line claimed by the Hungarians and that offered by the Czechs, and to decide whether or not the 1910 census offers a fair basis, His Majesty's Government are, in principle, in favour of the return to Hungary of those districts in which the population is predominantly Hungarian, subject possibly to certain modifications that may be desirable for economic reasons, e.g., Bratislava. The holding of plebiscites in those regions where the races are so ethnographically entangled and where there is a difference of opinion regarding the figures to be taken as a basis for the voting would, however, in the view of His Majesty's Government be extremely difficult, especially at such short notice as the Hungarian Government propose (before November 30.)

His Majesty's Government would, therefore, be happy to see the Czechs and Hungarians agree to settle their differences by reference to arbitration by the Italian and German Governments. If, however, it were deemed preferable or necessary that the question in dispute between the Czechoslovak and Hungarian Governments should be referred to the four Munich Powers, His Majesty's Government would be ready to take their part in trying to bring about an agreed settlement.

An expression of the views of His Majesty's Government on the above lines might, I feel, be welcome to Signor Mussolini as an indication that they are anxious to co-operate with him in the discussion of European questions. You will, of course, appreciate that His Majesty's Government do not wish to give the impression of trying to profit by any Italo-German disagreement over the future of Ruthenia.

Repeated to Berlin, Warsaw, Prague, Budapest, Bucharest, Belgrade and Paris No. 404.

34

British Prime Minister Neville Chamberlain
to Regent Miklós Horthy[1]

London, October 28, 1938

Dear Admiral Horthy:

I was very pleased to receive by the hand of Sir Thomas Moore the letter which Your Highness wrote to me on the 8th October, appealing for my support for your country's claims and referring to a conversation you had held with my brother.

I should like first of all to assure Your Highness that neither His Majesty's Government, nor myself are disinterested in the negotiations which your Government have been carrying on with the Czechoslovak Government for the purpose of adjusting the existing political frontier so as to bring it into closer harmony with the ethnic situation in that area. If we have abstained from intervention and comment upon the merits of the intricate problems which have been under discussion, it has not been from any indifference to the importance of the issues at stake. On the contrary it is our sincere desire that this opportunity should be taken to reach a settlement, inspired by good will and based on the rights and interests of all concerned, such as will lessen racial grievances and lay the foundations for a lasting and fruitful collaboration between Hungary and Czechoslovakia. As Your Highness may have seen Lord Halifax made it clear in a speech at Edinburgh on October 24th that His Majesty's Government recognise that Hungary has had legitimate claims and hope that means can be found, in peaceful negotiation, to give effect to them. I enclose the relevant extract.

I appreciate that difficulties have already arisen and may still arise during these negotiations but it has been and still is our hope that the two Governments most directly concerned may be able, with good will, patience, and moderation on both sides to reach a direct agreement.

Finally, I should like to say that, if at any time you feel that my good offices could be of service, I shall of course be very glad to do what lies in my power to help, in concert with the other parties to the Munich agreement, in reaching a solution of Hungary's claims such as will form the basis of an equitable settlement.

Yours sincerely,

Neville Chamberlain

---

[1]Horthy, *Confidential Papers*, pp. 109-11. The first and the last sentences of the letter were written by Chamberlain himself in ink.

ATTACHMENT

Passage Relating to the Czechoslovak-Hungarian Negotiations of the Speech of Lord Halifax at Edinburgh, October 24, 1938

The Hungarian Government are now in negotiation with the Czechoslovak Government, and we hope that they may reach an equitable solution, which will remove or lessen racial grievances. We recognise that Hungary has had legitimate claims, and we trust that means may be found to meet them.

There is no ideal solution of such problems, and there must always be minorities left on one side of the line or the other. But if the two parties can negotiate in a spirit of good will, and in the desire to find a remedy for clear grievances, we hope it may be possible for them to agree also on safeguards for minorities that will minimize injustice, and make more easy in future friendly cooperation between them.

35.

Note of the German Government to the Hungarian Government[1]

Budapest, Okt. 30, 1938.

Die Deutsche Regierung ist im Einvernehmen mit der Kgl. Italienischen Regierung bereit, dem Ersuchen der Kgl. Ungarischen Regierung bezüglich der Regelung des Problems der ungarischen Minderheiten in der Tschechoslowakei unter der Bedingung nachzukommen, dass die Kgl. Ungarische Regierung die bindende Erklärung abgibt, dass die Entscheidungen des durch Deutschland und Italien zu fällenden Schiedsspruchs als endgültige Regelung angenommen und gemäss den festzusetzen den Bestimmungen vorbehaltlos und unverzüglich durchgeführt werden.

Bejahendenfalls sind der deutsche und der kgl. italienische Aussenminister bereit, am 2. November d.J. in Wien zusammenzutreffen und namens ihrer Regierungen den Schiedsspruch zu fällen.

(unsigned)

---

[1]Magyar Tudományos Akadémia Történettudományi Intézete, *Diplomáciai iratok Magyarország külpolitikájához 1936-1945* (Budapest: Akadémiai Kiadó, 1962-   ), Vol. II, pp. 879-80. Hereafter cited as *Diplomáciai iratok*. Translated, the text reads: "The German Government, in accord with the Royal Italian Government, is ready to settle the problem of the Hungarian minority in Czechoslovakia as requested by the Royal Hungarian Government, on the condition that the Hungarian Government issue a binding declaration that the judgment arrived at by Germany and Italy will be accepted as final arbitration and that it will be carried out without reservation and without delay. In case of affirmation the German and the Royal Italian Foreign Ministers are ready to meet in Vienna on November 2 of the current year and bring about an arbitration in the name of their Governments."—The note was handed to Foreign Minister Kánya by the German Ambassador in Hungary, Erdmannsdorff.

36.

Note of the Italian Government to the Hungarian Government[1]

Budapest, Okt. 30, 1938.

L'Italie et l'Allemagne sont prêtes à accepter la demande d'arbitrage présentée par les Gouvernements de Budapest et de Prague à la condition que ledits Gouvernements déclarent officiellement que les décisions de l'arbitrage formulées par l'Italie et par l'Allemagne seront acceptées par les deux Gouvernements comme règlement définitif et exécutées en conformité de ce qui aura été décidé sans aucune réserve ou retard.

(unsigned)

---

[1]*Diplomáciai iratok*, II, 880. This note was handed to Foreign Minister Kánya by the Italian Ambassador in Hungary, Vinci.

37.

Documents on the Vienna Award[1]

MEMORANDUM ON THE CONFERENCE OF THE FOUR
FOREIGN MINISTERS IN THE BELVEDERE PALACE
ON NOVEMBER 2, 1938. FROM 12 NOON TO 2 P.M.

Present:

German Delegation
Foreign Minister von Ribbentrop
Under State Secretary Woermann
Counselor of Legation Altenburg
Minister Schmidt
Counselor of Legation Kordt
Czechoslovak Delegation
Foreign Minister Chvalkovský
Minister Krno

Italian Delegation
Foreign Minister Count Ciano
Ambassador Attolico
Minister Count Magistrati
Hungarian Delegation
Foreign Minister Kánya
Count Teleki, Minister of
Education

The Reich Foreign Minister opened the meeting with the following remarks:

"YOUR EXCELLENCIES, GENTLEMEN: I have the honor to welcome you in Vienna in the name of the Reich Government. I welcome especially my friend Count Ciano, Foreign Minister of Fascist Italy, as well as the Foreign Ministers of the Kingdom of Hungary and of Czechoslovakia.

---

[1]*German Documents*, IV. 118-127.

"The Kingdom of Hungary and Czechoslovakia have appealed to Germany and Italy to arbitrate on the frontier delimitation between their two countries.

"The Reich Government and the Royal Italian Government have responded to this appeal, and the Italian Foreign Minister and I have come here today to make this decision. I regard it as being of particular symbolic significance that Italy and Germany can devote themselves to this great and responsible task in this very house of Prince Eugene of Savoy. Two hundred years ago this prince of Italian blood, German statesman and general, once before brought freedom, peace and justice to peoples in southeastern Europe.

"Our task today is to determine the final frontier between Hungary and Czechoslovakia on an ethnographic basis and to find a solution of the questions connected with this. The arbitral award made by us is binding and final and is recognized in advance by Hungary and Czechoslovakia as the final settlement.

"The essential points of the views of both Governments are already known to us from previous negotiations. Nevertheless, I think it would serve a useful purpose if the representatives of both Governments briefly summarized their views on the question and stated their reasons, so that all arguments may be carefully considered again before the award is made.

"Before asking the representatives of the two Governments to speak, I first call on His Excellency the Italian Foreign Minister to address you."

Thereupon Count Ciano said as follows:

"YOUR EXCELLENCIES, GENTLEMEN: I have the honor to bid you welcome in the name of the Fascist Government.

"I wish to express to my friend Herr von Ribbentrop, Reich Foreign Minister, my sincere thanks for the cordial reception accorded to me here in Vienna, in the house of Prince Eugene, who, as the Reich Foreign Minister has said, brought freedom, peace, and justice to the peoples of southeastern Europe 200 years ago.

"And thus in accepting the role of arbiters at the request of the Hungarian and Czechoslovak Governments, the Rome-Berlin Axis has set itself the aim of adding a further important contribution to the many efforts already made for peace and reconstruction in Europe.

"I feel sure that our efforts will be crowned with success, and that from the meeting in Vienna there will arise a new order and a new era in central Europe, based on that international justice which we have always striven for and desired."

The Reich Foreign Minister then called upon M. Kánya, the Hungarian Foreign Minister, to speak.

M. Kánya began by expressing the thanks of the Hungarian Government to the German and Fascist Governments for their readiness to arbitrate in the territorial questions still outstanding between Hungary and Czechoslovakia. He intended to be brief, as all the facts were already in possession of the two Governments. Count Teleki, the Hungarian Minister of Education, would undertake to supplement his statements from the geographical and ethnographical angles. The Hungarian Government had endeavored to reach a friendly solution of the points at issue with Czechoslovakia by negotiation on the lines of the Munich Agreement of the four Great Powers. The Hungarian Government hoped that a settlement of this kind would also lead, above all, to an improvement of Hungarian-Czechoslovak relations. By preserving peace the Munich Agreement had rendered Europe a tremendous service. It had also contained the basis for a solution of the Hungarian-Czechoslovak question. It was true, the agreement had provided that the Hungarian-Czechoslovak question was to be settled within three months. To him this seemed a very long time, for it was a matter of importance to find a speedy solution. For this reason the Hungarian Government too had appealed to the German and Italian Governments to arbitrate and he was glad that this proposal had also been accepted by the Prague Government. Hungary had tried to reach direct agreement at first with the Czechoslovak Government at Komorn from October 9 to 13. When the negotiations were broken off, the Czechoslovak Government had made a further proposal, but great differences had still remained. For these disputed points, Hungary had proposed a decision by a court of arbitration or by a plebiscite. Hungary looked forward with a clear conscience to the arbitral award of the two powers and was convinced that the two Great Powers would give a just verdict, satisfactory to both parties.

Count Teleki, Minister of Education then stated that the Hungarian proposals were based upon purely ethnographic principles. The relevant facts were known and he had no need to go into details. The Munich Agreement had established two principles for the solution of the Hungarian-Czechoslovak question: first, the majority principle and second, the ruling that the year 1918 was to be the basis for counting the population, i.e. the last census prior to that date. It was a simple matter to draw a frontier on the basis of these principles. However the delineation of the frontier on purely ethnographic principles presented great difficulties at two points, first with regard to a rather large area around the town of Neutra, inhabited by a Hungarian majority and situated outside the actual ethnic frontier, and also with regard to the areas east of Kaschau. The Hungarian Government had proposed a special solution for these areas. It was also difficult to apply the ethnographic principle to the town of Pressburg. The difficulty here was that no one ethnic group possessed the absolute majority. Therefore the 50-percent principle was of no use here. It was true, however, that in 1911 there had been a relative Hungarian majority. It must also be taken into account that for centuries during the Turkish regime Pressburg had been the Hungarian capital; on the other hand, he admitted that the Slovaks must have access to the Danube. In conclusion, he would like to refer to several towns from Neutra to Munkacs which were close to the language frontier and which in 1918 had been 80-90 percent Hungarian but were later denationalized. Hungary therefore raised a claim to these towns on the ground of both ancient and recent rights.

Thereupon the Czechoslovak Foreign Minister spoke as follows:

"In the name of the Czechoslovak Government and at the same time in my own name I thank Your Excellency for the kind words which you have just addressed to me.

"In the person of Your Excellency and of His Excellency Count Ciano, the Italian Foreign Minister, I greet the representatives of those two Great Powers, who for 2 years have been showing the rest of the world the true and the shortest way to a new and better foreign policy.

"The fact that the two Foreign Ministers have accepted the role of arbiters in the question of the Hungarian minority in Slovakia is a fresh proof of the firm and solid resolution of the policy pursued by Berlin and Rome to contribute to the pacification of an important part of central Europe by as speedy and just decision as possible.

"We have come to Vienna with complete confidence in the objectivity of the Great Powers toward us.

"On the occasion of the dinner given in Berlin on September 28, 1937, in honor of His Excellency the Head of the Italian Government, His Excellency the Reich Chancellor said that the cooperation of Germany and Italy not only served the common interest of the two Great Powers but in actual fact served the aim of speedy and general understanding among the nations of Europe.

"His Excellency the Duce answered on that occasion that Germany and Italy were prepared to work together with all other peoples of good will.

"I take advantage of this very opportunity to state solemnly here that the Slovak, Ruthenian, and Czech peoples desired to demonstrate just this good will by addressing Your Excellencies' Governments the request which will be the subject of your decision today.

"If we demand respect and full consideration for our own claims, it is with the intention of applying the same standards to the Hungarian people, too. With all our hearts we hope that your award today in this historic palace with its symbolic name will lay the firm foundations from which we will be able to face the future with complete confidence.

"May you by your award make it possible for us to return home from Vienna conscious that as a result of your award we may let bygones be bygones in our common relations with our neighbor Hungary, and may this meeting in the Belvedere become a historic act which will open up for the two neighboring peoples a new, bright, and wide outlook into the future which, with God's help, may be a better one.

"With your consent, Minister Krno will answer Count Teleki's statements and briefly put before you the Czechoslovak point of view."

Minister Krno then made the following statement:

"The Munich Agreement of September 29, 1938, which introduced a new era in central Europe and particularly in the history of my country, specified a period of 3 months for the settlement by direct negotiations of the question of the Hungarian and Polish minorities in Czechoslovakia. The Czechoslovak Government honestly endeavored to carry out faithfully this point of the Munich Agreement also. As early as October 9, that is, 10 days after the Munich meeting, it took part in the negotiations in Komorn and tried to reach a settlement. It was and still is prepared to accept the nationality principle as the basis of the new frontier delimitation.

"At Komorn, however, the Hungarian delegation submitted a proposal which in Czechoslovakia's view could not form a basis for national justice. The Result of this proposal would have been to replace the present Hungarian minority in Czechoslovakia (approximately 700,000) by a new and almost as numerous Slav (Slovak and Ruthenian) minority in Hungary.

"The negotiations in Komorn were then declared by the Hungarian delegation to be at an end.

"On October 22 my government handed over in Budapest a new proposal offering to resume direct negotiations at once on this general basis. The Hungarian Government did not see its way to accept this offer.

"Thereupon the Hungarian Government made a counterproposal to solve the question by means of a plebiscite or arbitration. Fully relying on the sense of justice of the German and Italian Governments, the Czechoslovak Government accepted this proposal. In the negotiations with Hungary, the Czechoslovak Government upheld the view that a solution must be found by which Hungary would receive a number of Slovaks and Ruthenians equal to the number of Hungarians who would remain in the Czechoslovak state. On the basis of Czechoslovak statistics for 1930, however, the Hungarian proposals would have left only 110,000 Magyars in Czechoslovakia, compared with over 200,000 Slovaks and Ruthenians who would have fallen to Hungary. It was moreover to be remembered that two or three times hundred thousand Slovaks already were living in Hungary as a minority. The starting point for solution of the question must be the compact ethnic area *(Volksboden)*. The Hungarian side has stated that the Munich principles must be applied uniformly, but in actual fact, conditions in Bohemia and Moravia could not be compared with those in Slovakia and Carpatho-Ukraine.[2] In Bohemia and Moravia the ethnic frontier had been unchanged for a long time, and consequently Germany had been able to claim that, in the areas to be ceded, an ancient German cultural area was involved. Teleki, the Hungarian Minister of Education, had stated that Hungary's demands were based on ancient and recent rights. He felt that he must raise objections to this claim. If the year 1910 were taken as a basis, there perhaps existed Hungarian majorities in many places, but if one went back only 20 to 30 years and took the census of 1880, quite different results were obtained. In 1910 for example, Kaschau had had a small Hungarian majority, but in 1880 the town had been predominantly Slovak. Thus his view that Hungary could demand these towns on the ground of ancient and recent rights was not quite correct for, if one ignores the last 30 years, the Slovak side could demand with equal justice that the 1880 figures should be taken into consideration. Even in 1910 Kaschau had been a Hungarian-language enclave in a compact Slovak ethnic area."

Kánya, the Hungarian Foreign Minister, replied to this that in his opinion the Czechoslovak Government was adhering too strictly to the Munich Agreement, which had provided a period of 3 months for the solution of these questions. The Munich Agreement had only this one fault, namely, that the period of 3 months was too long, for, if the question were allowed to drag on for so long, a peaceful solution would no longer be possible. From his own experience he could say that tension in Hungary during the last few weeks had reached an unbearable pitch, and reports in his possession from Czechoslovakia gave the same picture. In all probability matters would have come to an armed conflict, and the Hungarian Government had therefore appealed to Germany and Italy to arbitrate.

Count Teleki, the Minister of Education, stated that the principles established by Minister Krno would create entirely new problems. Hungary had been aiming at a territorial solution. Poland had done the same. In addition, Hungarian claims were made on a historical basis. The proposal made at Komorn by the Czechoslovak Government to add to Hungary a number of Slovaks equal to the number of Hungarians remaining in Czechoslovakia, in order to establish a balance, could

---

[2]Ruthenia

127

not be recognized. For one thing it must be taken into consideration that in a very short space of time this balance might again be disturbed by emigration or an important increase of population. In the long run, the application of this principle was not calculated to establish friendly relations, and therefore at Komorn this principle had been described by Hungary as one of mutual hostages. For the rest, Hungary recognized the principle of the compact ethnic area. However, at two points, i.e. at Neutra and Kaschau, the great change in nationalities (Volkstum) in the course of time must be recognized. It had been pointed out by the Czechoslovak side that between 1880 and 1911 these towns had been Magyarized. But if one went further back, it was seen that until 1880 there had been a Slovakization, and in earlier years, as shown, for example, by the statistics of 1720, this had been an old Hungarian ethnic and settlement area. The grandfathers of the inhabitants now described as Slovaks had still been, for the most part, Hungarians, as could be seen today to some extent from their names. It was true that Neutra and Kaschau were language enclaves if the 50-percent principle was taken as a basis. However he wished to point out that Kaschau, for example, was separated from the compact Hungarian ethnic area by a few small communities inhabited by Magyars to a maximum of 45 percent and an average of 37.8 percent.

Foreign Minister Chvalkovský stated that he fully agreed with Foreign Minister Kánya's view regarding the necessity of a speedy solution. He asked, however, that the views of Tiso, the Slovak Prime Minister, and Volosin, the Ukrainian Prime Minister, on Count Teleki's statements should first be heard. Reich Foreign Minister von Ribbentrop said that they had met to find a solution for a Slovak-Hungarian question. The views of both Governments had been expressed by their Foreign Ministers. He could therefore see no point in hearing the views of a number of additional experts on the subject, for as such he must regard Tiso and Volosin, especially as the problem itself was sufficiently familiar to both arbiters. He therefore did not think that the circle of participants in today's conference should be enlarged.

He would take the liberty of saying the following on the subject of Foreign Minister Kánya's remarks that too long a period had been fixed by the Munich Agreement; it was a result of the cooperation of the German and Italian Governments with the two other Powers at Munich that the question of the Hungarian minority had been brought near to solution at all. Moreover, the two Governments had stated their willingness to undertake the role of arbiter in this question so that it might be brought to a peaceful and speedy solution. He had noted with interest the statements of the Czechoslovak and Hungarian delegations. The preparatory talks for the arbitral award could thus be regarded as ended. The problem has been expounded with sufficient clarity. As for MM. Tiso and Volosin, they would have an opportunity for unofficial talks with the two arbiters in the course of the lunch to which both of them had also been invited.

After lunch, the Italian and German delegations would then enter into consultations on the award to be made, which would probably be completed late in the afternoon. He would then ask the Hungarian and Czechoslovak delegates to attend a final meeting in the Belvedere Palace.

Foreign Minister Count Ciano expressed agreement with this proposal. Foreign Minister Chvalkovský then asked to be allowed to speak again. In view of the thoroughness which he had learned in German schools, he asked if he might point out the following: MM. Tiso and Volosin could not be described as experts. The Slovak Prime Minister had been the leader of the Slovak delegation which had up to now negotiated with the Hungarians. M. Volosin was Prime Minister of the Ukraine. He therefore asked that in any minutes of the meeting to be drawn up the two gentlemen should not be referred to as experts. Reich Minister von Ribbentrop and Foreign Minister Count Ciano expressed their agreement.

Thereupon the meeting adjourned.

E. Kordt

II.

MEMORANDUM ON THE ANNOUNCEMENT OF THE ARBITRAL AWARD IN THE PRESENCE OF THE FOUR FOREIGN MINISTERS ON NOVEMBER 2, 1938, AT 7 P.M.

Reich Foreign Minister von Ribbentrop opened the meeting by stating that the German and Italian Governments had now completed their task of arbitrating in the question of the cession of Czechoslovak territory to Hungary. The task of the arbiters had been extremely difficult. But on the basis of the ethnographic principle a decision had been reached, which, if correctly carried out, would bring a lasting and just solution of the questions outstanding between Hungary and Czechoslovakia.

Count Ciano corroborated this statement on behalf of the Italian Government. He said that the arbitration by the German and Italian Governments had again revealed the solidarity of the Axis. He, too, wished to stress the difficulty of the task undertaken by the two Governments and to call attention to the efforts of both to find a lasting and just solution of the problem, designed to introduce a new era and to lay the foundations for friendly and good neighborly relations between Hungary and Czechoslovakia.

Then followed the reading and afterward the signing of the arbitral award and accompanying protocol. Thereupon Reich Foreign Minister von Ribbentrop declared the meeting closed.

E. Kordt

III.

Vienna, November 2, 1938

Pol. IV 7958.

ARBITRAL AWARD

In virtue of a request from the Royal Hungarian Government and the Czechoslovak Government to the German and Royal Italian Governments to settle by award the questions pending between them relating to territories to be ceded to Hungary, as well as in the virtue of notes thereupon exchanged on October 30, 1938, between the Governments concerned, the German Foreign Minister, Herr Joachim Von Ribbentrop, and the Foreign Minister of His Majesty the King of Italy, Emperor of Ethiopia, Count Galeazzo Ciano, have met this day in Vienna, and, after further discussion with the Royal Hungarian Foreign Minister, M. Kálmán Kánya, and the Czechoslovak Foreign Minister, Dr. František Chvalkovský, have promulgated the following award:

1. The areas to be ceded to Hungary by Czechoslovakia are marked on the annexed map.[3] Demarkation of the frontier on the spot is delegated to a Hungarian-Czechoslovak Commission.

2. The evacuation by Czechoslovakia of the areas to be ceded and their occupation by Hungary begins on November 5, 1938, and is to be completed by November 10, 1938. The detailed stages of the evacuation and occupation, as well as other procedures connected therewith, are to be settled at once by a Hungarian-Czechoslovak Commission.

3. The Czechoslovak Government will insure that the territories to be ceded are left in an orderly condition at the time of evacuation.

4. Special questions arising out of the cession of territory, in particular questions relating to nationality and option, are to be regulated by a Hungarian-Czechoslovak Commission.

5. Likewise, special measures for the protection of persons of the Magyar nationality remaining in Czechoslovak territory and of persons not of the Magyar race in the ceded territories are to be agreed upon by a Hungarian-Czechoslovak Commission. This commission will take special care that the Magyar ethnic group (Volksgruppe) in Pressburg be accorded the same status as other ethnic groups there.

---

[3] The map attached to this Appendix is not identical to that mentioned in the document.

6. Insofar as disadvantages and difficulties in the sphere of economics or (railway) traffic may be caused by the cession of territory to Hungary for the area remaining to Czechoslovakia, the Hungarian Government will, in agreement with the Czechoslovak Government, do its utmost to remove these disadvantages and difficulties.

7. In the event of difficulties or doubts arising from the implementation of this award, the Royal Hungarian and Czechoslovak Governments will settle the matter directly between themselves. Should they, however, fail to reach agreement on any question, this question will then be submitted to the German and Italian Governments for final decision.

Joachim von Ribbentrop

Galeazzo Ciano

IV

The general course of the new frontier between the Kingdom of Hungary and the Republic of Czechoslovakia as determined in the award made by the German Foreign Minister and the Royal Italian Minister for Foreign Affairs on November 2, 1938, is as follows:

Starting from the old frontier south of Pressburg, the new frontier runs north of the Pressburg-Neuhäusl railway line, turns in a northeasterly direction to the northwest of Neuhäusl, and is continued north of Vráble direct to the Lewenz-Altsohl railway line. The towns of Neuhäusl and Lewenz revert to Hungary. To the east of Lewenz the frontier runs diagonally through the Eipel territory some 30 kilometers north of the old frontier. Its further course is directly to the north of the towns Lutschenetz and Gross-Steffelsdorf, which also revert to Hungary. The frontier then turns to the northeast, taking in the town of Jolschva, and in the neighborhood of Rosenau extends direct to the German-settlement area of the Unterzips. It then turns north, includes Kaschau in Hungarian territory, and follows a southeasterly course to a point some 30 kilometers north of the railway junction of Sátoraljaujhely on the former Hungarian frontier. It then proceeds due east to a point directly north of Ungvár, which is assigned to Hungary. The frontier then takes a sharp turn to the southeast. Its further course passes close to the north of Munkatsch. Continuing in a southeasterly direction, the new frontier links up with the old frontier northeast of the Rumanian-frontier railway station of Halmei.

Of the disputed towns, therefore, Pressburg itself, the capital of Slovakia, the old cathedral town of Neutra, and the town of Sevljusch in the Carpatho-Ukraine, with its surrounding villages, remain within the Czechoslovak republic. The towns of Neuhäusl, Lewenz, Lutschenetz, Kaschau, Užhorod, and Munkatsch were adjudged to the Kingdom of Hungary.

The new ruling returns the whole area of compact Hungarian settlement to the Kingdom of Hungary. At points where circumstances did not allow an exact determination of the frontier on ethnic lines *(Volksmässige Grenzziehung),* the interests of both sides were carefully weighed.

38.

Protocol concerning the Arbitral Award Establishing the Czechoslovak-Hungarian boundary.

Signed at Vienna, Nov. 2, 1938.

(Entered into force same day. Not registered with the Secretariat of the League of Nations.)[1]

In pursuance of the request made by the Royal Hungarian and the Czechoslovak Governments to the German and the Royal Italian Governments to settle by arbitration the outstanding question of the areas to be ceded to Hungary, and in pursuance of the notes exchanged on the subject between the Governments concerned on October 30th, 1938, the German Reich Minister of Foreign Affairs, Herr Joachim von Ribbentrop, and the Minister of Foreign Affairs of His Majesty the King of Italy and Emperor of Ethiopia, Count Galeazzo Ciano, have today met at the Belvedere Castle of Vienna and given the desired arbitral award in the names of their Governments.

For this purpose they have invited to Vienna the Royal Hungarian Minister of Foreign Affairs, M. Koloman von Kánya, and the Czechoslovak Minister of Foreign Affairs, Dr. Franz Chvalkovský, in order to give them an opportunity in the first place again to explain the point of view of their Governments.

This arbitral award, together with the map mentioned in paragraph 1, has been handed to the Royal Hungarian Minister of Foreign Affairs and to the Czechoslovak Minister of Foreign Affairs. They have taken cognizance of it and have again confirmed, on behalf of their Governments, the statement which they made on October 30th, 1938, that they accept the arbitral award as a final settlement and that they undertake to carry it out unconditionally and without delay.

Done in the German and Italian languages in quadruplicate.

Vienna, November 2nd, 1938.

  v. Ribbentrop   *Count Ciano*   *v. Kánya*   *Chvalkovský*

---

[1]Hudson. *International Legislation,* VIII. 201.

NOTES EXCHANGED BETWEEN THE
CZECHOSLOVAK AND HUNGARIAN GOVERNMENTS

39.

Note hongroise, ler octobre 1938[1]

7/1 - 1938   Prague, le ler octobre 1938.

Monsieur le Ministre,

Par ordre de mon Gouvernement, j'ai l'honneur de communiquer à Votre Excellence ce qui suit:

Les décisions de Munich ayant créé une situation nouvelle, mon Gouvernement invite le Gouvernement de la République Tchécoslovaque à entamer immédiatement des négociations directs, afin que le droit des nationalités à disposer d'elles-mêmes soit réalisé en toute égalité de droit avec celui des Allemands des Sudetes.

La poursuite la plus rapide de ces négociations et, autant que faire se peut, leur conclusion en base d'un accord mutuel est non seulement dans l'intérêt des bonnes relations des deux Pays, mais aussi dans celui de toute l'Europe. C'est pourquoi le Governement Royal Hongrois prie Votre Excellence de lui faire savoir de toute urgence quand et où le Gouvernement de la République Tchécoslovaque désire commencer lesdites négociations.

Veuillez agréer, Monsieur le Ministre, les assurances de ma très haute considération.

Wettstein

---

[1]*La Documentation.* p. 25.

40

Communiqué de 2 octobre du Gouvernement Tchécoslovaque[1]

En relation avec la pression exercée sur la Tchécoslovaquie pour que les régions frontières à majorité allemande soient rattachées à l'Allemagne, le Gouvernement hongrois a fait ces jours-ci, par l'intermédiaire de son ministre à Prague, une démarche et a demandé pour les hongrois de Tchécoslovaquie les mêmes avantages que ceux accordés aux Allemands des Sudètes.

Le Gouvernement hongrois se référait aux déclarations de nos hommes d'État, selon lesquelles nous voulons accorder aux Hongrois de Tchécoslovaquie les mêmes droits qu'aux Allemands.

Il a été répondu au Gouvernement hongrois que ces déclarations pouvaient se rapporter au traitement des minorités nationales dans le cadre de l'État, tandis que les négociations internationales sur la question sudète se développaient sur une base tout à fait différente. En même temps, le Gouvernement hongrois a reçu l'assurance que le Gouvernement tchécoslovaque veut accorder aux Hongrois de Tchécoslovaquie tous les droits contenus dans le statut nationaliste élaboré au cours des négociations avec les Allemands de Tchécoslovaquie.

Le Gouvernement hongrois ne s'est pas contenté de ces déclarations et a demandé que les Hongrois de Tchécoslovaquie aient les mêmes droits de disposer d'eux-mêmes que les Allemands de Tchécoslovaquie.

Les décisions des quatre puissances occidentales, à Munich, ont pris note de ces demandes de nos Hongrois et nous avons été en même temps forcés, sur la base du droit de libre disposition, de céder non seulement les régions à majorité allemands, mais aussi celles à majorité polonaise.

Dans cet état de choses, le Gouvernement tchécoslovaque n'a pas pu rejeter le voeu du Gouvernement hongrois, demandant qu'on s'entende sur l'application du droit de libre disposition à la minorité hongroise.

Les négociations à ce sujet seront confinés a une Commission spéciale hungaro-tchécoslovaque qui commencera ses travaux ces jours-ci.

---

[1]*La Documentation*, p. 27.

41.

Note hongroise, 3 octobre, 1938[1]

8/1 - 1938   Prague, le 3 octobre, 1938

Monsieur le Ministre,

D'ordre de mon Gouvernement, j'ai l'honneur de communiquer à Votre Excellence ce que suit:

Le Gouvernement Royal Hongrois attache de l'importance à ce que les négociations avec le Gouvernement de la République Tchécoslovaque puissent se dérouler dans une atmosphère et un esprit amicaux. C'est pourquoi il tient pour nécessaire que—dans le but de créer une atmosphère pacifique—certaines conditions soient préalablement remplies.

Partant, le Gouvernement Royal Hongrois invite le Gouvernement de la République Tchécoslovaque à prendre sans délai les mesures suivantes:

1. Libérer immédiatement les prisonniers politiques hongrois;

2. Démobiliser sans retard les soldats de nationalité hongroise et leur permettre de rentrer chez eux;

3. Constituer pour la protection de la vie et des biens, ainsi que pour le maintien de l'ordre local, des détachements sous commandement mixte;

4. Remettre à la Hongrie, en signe de la cession symbolique de territoires, deux ou trois villes tchécoslovaques limitrophes de la frontière, lesquelles villes seront occupées par les troupes hongroises. — Viennent en considération comme telles dans la partie ouest: Komárom ou Párkánynána ou Ipolyság; dans la partie est: la gare de Sátoraljaujhely ou Csap ou Beregszász; enfin

5. Le Gouvernement Royal Hongrois propose que les négociations hungaro-tchécoslovaques directes soient entamées à Komárom jeudi, le 6 courant, à 4 heures de l'après-midi.

La délegation hongroise sera personnellement présidée par Son Excellence M. de Kánya, ministre des Affaires Etrangères de Hongrie.

Veuillez agréer, Monsieur le Ministre, etc . . .

Wettstein

---

[1]*La Documentation*, pp. 25-26.

42.

Note hongroise, 5 octobre, 1938[1]

11/b - 1938.   Prague, le 5 octobre 1938.

Monsieur le Ministre,

Par ordre de mon Gouvernement, j'ai l'honneur de faire savoir à Votre Excellence que le Gouvernement Royal Hongrois est surpris de ne pas avoir la réponse que Son Excellence M. Krofta a promise pour hier le 4 courant en réponse à la note No. 8/I - 1938 que le Gouvernement Royal Hongrois Lui a fait remettre par le Ministre de Hongrie en date du 3 courant.

Le Gouvernement Royal Hongrois demande une réponse immédiate.

J'ai en outre l'honneur, d'ordre de mon Gouvernement, de protester énergiquement contre le traitement et les persécutions auxquels sont livrés les hongrois en Tchécoslovaquie, — circonstance qui met en danger les bonnes relations entre les deux Pays et compromet l'avenir de celles-ci.

Il est naturel que les Hongrois en Tchécoslovaquie vivent actuellment dans un état d'agitation et, connaissant les décisions de Munich, attendent avec une angoisse redoublée l'application de celles-ci.

Ces circonstances aussi exigent impérativement la mise à exécution immédiate des règlements nécessaires.

Veuillez agréer, Monsieur le Ministre, etc . . .

Vörnle, chargé d'Affaires a.i.

---

[1]*La Documentation*, p. 26.

43.

Note tchécoslovaque, 5 octobre 1938[1]

Ministerstvo Zahranicnich Veci.   No. 140504/II-1/38.

A la Légation Royale de Hongrie, Praha.

Par sa note no. 8/I-1938 en date du 3 courant, la Légation Royale a bien voulu demander entre autre la libération immédiate des prisonniers politiques hongrois.

Comme suite à la communication orale qui a été faite ce matin à M. Le Chargé d'Affaires de Hongrie, le Ministére des Affaires Etrangères a l'honneur de faire savoir à la Légation Royale que dans son désir de donner une preuve immédiate de sa bonne volonté le Gouvernement Tchécoslovaque vient de donner les ordres necessaires pour la libération

---

[1]*La Documentation*, P. 26.

sans retard de tous les prisonniers pour lesquels cette libération peut être ordonnée par la voie administrative. Pour les autres cas, une amnistie est déjà en préparation.

Le Ministère des Affaires Etrangères saisit cette occasion pour renouveler les assurances de sa haute consideration.

Praha, le 5 octobre 1938.

(Sceau.)

44.

Note hongroise, 6 octobre 1938[1]

15/b - 1938   Prague, le 6 octobre 1938.

Monsieur le Ministre,

J'ai l'honneur de communiquer à Votre Excellence que, vu la crise gouvernementale tchécoslovaque, le Gouvernement Royal Hongrois consent à remettre le commencement des négociations à samedi le 8 courant, à 12 heures.

Le Gouvernement Royal Hongrois maintient invariablement les postulats formulés dans sa note No. 8/I - 1938 du 3 courant.

Le Gouvernement Royal Hongrois attire l'attenetion du Gouvernement Tchécoslovaque sur ce que la situation des Hongrois en Tchécoslovaquie est de plus en plus intenable du fait de son incertitude et que cette circonstance aussi exige la poursuite rapide des négociations.

Veuillez agréer, Monsieur le Ministre, etc . . .

Vörnle

---

[1]*La Documentation*, p. 26.

45.

Note hongroise, 7 octobre 1938[1]

21/b - 1938   Prague, le 7 octobre 1938.

Monsieur le Ministre,

D'ordre de mon Gouvernement, j'ai l'honneur de communiquer à Votre Excellence que chaque jour de retard en ce qui concerne le commencement des négociations représente une grande perte. C'est pourquoi le Gouvernement Royal Hongrois persiste à maintenir le samedi 8 courant comme date du commencement des négociations.

---

[1]*La Documentation*, p. 26.

Vu cependant le changement qui a eu lieu dans la personne du Ministre des Affaires Etrangères de la République Tchécoslovaque et la déclaration que celui-ci à faite à Rome, selon laquelle il désire poursuivre les négociations sans retard et le plus rapidement possible, le Ministre des Affaires Etrangères de Hongrie accepte comme tout dernier terme pour le commencement des négociations le dimanche 9 courant, 7 heures du soir.

Afin que lesdites négociations puissent avoir lieu dans l'atmosphère pacifique désirée, le Gouvernement Royal Hongrois réitère ici sa demande pour que les postulats formulés dans sa note No. 8/I - 1938 du 3 courant et qui n'auraient pas encore été effectués, le soient sans retard.

Le Gouvernement Royal Hongrois présume que le Gouvernement de la République Tchécoslovaque a accepté sa proposition visant à ce que les négociations aient lieu à Komárom et demande une confirmation à ce sujet.

Veuillez agréer, Monsieur le Ministre, etc . . .

Wettstein

46.

Note tchécoslovaque, 7 octobre 1938[1]

Le Gouvernement tchécoslovaque est d'accord pour que les négociations directes. hungaro-tchécoslovaques commencent le 9 octobre, à 19 heures.

La délégation tchécoslovaque sera composée comme suit:

S.E.M. le Ministre Josef Tiso, chef de la délégation;

S.E.M. le Ministre Jan Durčansky,

S.E.M. le Ministre Ivan Ihnatij Párkányi, membres de la délégation;

S.E.M. le Ministre plénipotentiaire Dr. Ivan Krno, conseiller diplomatique de la délégation.

La délégation aura le plein pouvoir nécessaire pour discuter dès le début des négociations les quatre points mentionnés dans la note du Gouvernement hongrois du 3 octobre 1938.

Praha, le 7 octobre 1938.

---

[1]*La Documentation*, p. 26. In fact, the composition of the delegation was different; see "Negotiations in Komárom," in Chapter III, above.

47.

Communication hongroise a Berlin, Londres, Paris, Rome et Varsovie, 14 octobre 1938[1]

Le Gouvernement Royal de Hongrie, conformément au contenu du Protocole additionel signé à Munich le 30 septembre 1938 par les Chefs des Gouvernements de l'Allemagne, de la France, de la Grande-Bretagne et de l'Italie, a fait remettre au Gouvernement de la République Tchéco-slovaque le 1er octobre dernier une note demandant l'ouverture immédiate de négociations amicales en vue de la mise en valeur du droit des nationalités à disposer d'elles-mêmes, comme elle a été réalisée au cours du règlement des réclamations des Allemands des Sudètes. Cette note n'a pas manqué de souligner que l'aboutissement rapide des négociations ainsi proposées était dans l'intérêt non seulement des deux Pays mêmes, mais aussi dans celui de l'Europe entière.

Dans une deuxième note remise au Gouvernement de Prague, le 3 octobre courant, le Gouvernement Royal de Hongrie a proposé le 6 octobre comme date de la réunion des deux délégations.

Le Gouvernement tchécoslovaque, en invoquant certains événements d'ordre politique intérieure, a demandé la remise de cette réunion pour le 9 octobre.

Les propositions hongroises ont été transmises à la Délégation slovaque au cours de la premiere séance qui a eu lieu à cette date dans la soirée.

Le Délégation slovaque s'est servie de différents prétextes pour retarder la remise d'une réponse méritoire. Elle a allégué même son ignorance de la metiére pour ne répondre aux propositions hongroises que le 12 courant.

La première contre-proposition de la Délégation slovaque a eu plutot l'air d'une moquerie. Elle s'est bornée notamment à offrir l'autonomie pour les Hongrois habitant le territoire actuel de la Slovaquie. Sur le refus ferme et net de M. de Kánya de négocier dans ces conditions, la Délégation slovaque s'est décidée à proposer la rétrocession de l'île de "Csallóköz," ce qui ne represente qu'une partie infime des territoires que le Gouvernement hongrois a indiqués comme étant à céder en vertu des décisions de Munich.

Sur ces entrefaites les deux délégations se sont séparées avec l'intention de se reunir hier matin et de s'occuper de nouvelles propositions tchécoslovaques qui, cette fois-ci, auraient dû s'étendre sur tout le long de la frontière hungaro-tchécoslovaque.

---

[1]La Documentation, pp. 28-29.

Malhereusement, ces nouvelles propositions de la Délégation slovaque n'ont marqué qu'un faible progrés sur les anciennes. Elles se şont réduites à des rectifications de frontiére d'un certaine importance, mais elles refusaient à la Hongrie la rétrocession de toutes les villes importantes à majorité hongroise des territoires en litige.

Un coup d'oeil sur les cartes et quelques commentaires de la Délégation slovaque suffisaient à convaincre la Délégation hongroise que les negociateurs de la Tchécoslovaquie sont moins guidés par les principes ethniques qui se trouvent à base de l'arrangement de Munich, que par des considérations d'ordre stratégique et économique et par d'autres, motivées par les intérêts de la politique de communications ferroviaires.

Il es évident que la Délégation hongroise ne pouvait admettre une argumentation tout à fait contraire aux principes qui ont commandé même dans les détails le règlement des revendications allemandes et polonaises.

En effet, la Délégation hongroise s'est basée sur les statistiques résultant du recensement de 1910, vu que le règlement du différend germano-tchécoslovaque a trouvé sa solution sur une base analogue. Mais la Délégation hongroise a même réussi à démontrer que les contre-propositions tchécoslovaques ne correspondaient même pas aux statistiques tendacieuses tchèques de 1930, préparées dans l'intérêt du nouveau régime et portant les marques des expatriations et d'une dénationalisation systématique.

Il ressort clairement de ce qui précède que la Délégation tchécoslovaque refusait d'appliquer le principe fondamental du traitement analogue des revendications hongroises avec celles des Allemands et des Polonais. En effet, une discrimination évidente au détriment de la Hongrie était à la base de toutes les propositions et argumentations de la Délégation tchécoslovaque.

Au seuil de la dernière réunion, la Délégation hongroise s'est vu confirmée dans son soupçon que la tactique dilatoire de la Délégation slovaque ne sert que de gagne-temps en vue du regroupement de l'armée tchécoslovaque. D'après les informations du Gouvernement hongrois, les mouvements des troupes tchécoslovaques, au cours des dernier jours, sont devenus de plus en plus symptomatiques et les manoeuvres des négociateurs se sont dévoilées l'après-midi même de la dernière réunion du 13 au soir.

Ce n'est pas une personnalité moins importante que l'expert militaire même de la Délégation slovaque qui a tenu à prononcer un discours menaçant devant le micro de la station de radio-diffusion de Presbourg et ce discours fut suivi d'un belliqueux appel aux citoyens et aux soldats.

Au lieu d'extorquer des concessions à la Délégation hongroise, — comme il en était évidemment le but—ces manifestations ont eu pour seul résultat de déterminer la Délégation hongroise à interrompre ces négociations absolument vaines où l'esprit conciliateur des arrangements de Munich a perdu tout terrain.

En outre, l'attitude provocatrice adoptée par le Gouvernement de la Tchécoslovaquie a obligé le Gouvernement hongrois à prendre les mesures militaires que commandait la situation ansi créée et les intérêts capitaux qui s'attachent à la sécurité du pays.

Le Gouvernement Royal de hongrie ayant l'honneur de porter à la connaissance du Gouvernement . . . les evénéments qui viennent de se dérouler, ose espérer que la marche des négociations hungaro-tchéco-slovaques ne manquera pas de convaincre le Gouvernement . . . qu'une solution rapide s'impose sur la base du droit d'égalité en face du traite-ment dont ont profité l'Allemagne et la Pologne. Le Gouvernement Royal désire confier à la sagesse du Gouvernement . . . la suite qu'il voudra bien donner à ce qui précède.

48.

Note hongroise, 22 octobre 1938[1]

37/b - 1938   Prague, le 22 octobre 1938

Monsieur le Ministre,

Me réferant à la communication de Votre Excellence en date du 20 octobre, selon laquelle le Ministre d'Allemagne à Budapest trans-mettra l'après-midi du même jour au Gouvernement Hongrois le projet sur lequel se sont mise d'accord les membres de la Délégation tchéco-slovaque, MM. Tiso, Durčansky et Bačinsky, au cours de leurs conversa-tions à Munich avec S.E.M. le Ministre von Ribbentrop, j'ai l'honneur, d'ordre de mon Gouvernement, de communiquer à Votre Excellence ce qui suit:

Le Ministre d'Allemagne à Budapest a présenté le -20 courant la carte, élaborée en base des conversations ayant eu lieu à Munich entre MM. von Ribbentrop et Tiso et faisant ressortir la nouvelle proposition tchécoslovaque.

M. von Erdmannsdorff a remarqué à cette occasion que la propo-sition officielle serait faite par le Gouvernement Tchécoslovaque lui-même, qui me la remettrait.

---

[1]*La Documentation*, p. 29.

En remarquant que ce qui précède ne concorde pas entièrement avec la communication que Votre Excellence a bien voulu me faire le 20 courant, j'ai l'honneur de faire savoir à Votre Excellence que le Gouvernement Royal Hongrois attend au plus tôt la proposition du Gouvernement Tchécoslovaque.

Veuillez agréer, Monsieur le Ministre, etc . . .

Wettstein

49.

Note tcnécoslovaque, 22 octobre 1938[1]

No. 150.095/II-1/38   Praha, le 22 octobre 1938

Monsieur le Ministre,

En réponse à votre lettre no. 37/b - 1938 du 22 octobre 1938, j'ai l'honneur de vous faire parvenir ci-jointe la carte faisant ressortir la nouvelle proposition officielle de mon Gouvernement.

La ligne marquée sur cette carte devrait servir de base générale pour les nouvelles négociations. auxquelles resteraient réservées les modifications ultérieures.[2]

Veuillez agréer, Monsieur le Ministre, etc . . .

Signature

---

[1]*La Documentation*, p. 29.

[2]L'offre tchécoslovaque No. 3 (22 octobre 1938) prévoyait la cession de 11.300 km^2 où le recensement de 1910 avait enregistre 740.000 habitants dont 680.000 Hongrois, et le recensement de 1930, 850.000 habitants.

50.

Note hongroise, 24 octobre 1938[1]

39/biz.   Prague, le 24 octobre 1938

Monsieur le Ministre,

J'ai l'honneur d'accuser réception de la Note No. 150.095/II-1/1938, en date du 22 octobre, par laquelle Votre Excellence a bien voulu me faire parvenir une carte faisant ressortir la nouvelle proposition officielle du Gouvernement Tchécoslovaque devant servir de base générale pour les nouvelles négociations auxquelles resteraient réservées les modifications ultérieures. Je n'ai pas manqué de soumettre immédiatement cette note à mon gouvernement d'ordre duquel je me permets de communiquer à Votre Excellence ce qui suit:

---

[1]*La Documentation*, pp. 29-30.

1. Le Gouvernement Royal de Hongrie constate avec satisfaction qu'un accord subsiste entre des deux Gouvernements pour une partie considérable du territoire revendiqué. La remise à la Hongrie de cette territoire ne saurait être retardée plus longtemps. C'est pourquoi le Gouvernement Royal de Hongrie propose de procéder à la prise en possession de ce territoire, y compris les communes de Tótmegyer, Komáromcsehi, Komáromszemere et Andrási par les troupes hongroises à partir du 27 octobre courant. L'occupation du territoire en question pourrait être effectuée en trois jours.

2. Des différences subsistent néanmoins qui sont substantielles et concernent moins l'étendue que surtout l'importance du territoire à rétrocéder. Ces différences se rapportent principalement à des villes qui, à l'exception de Presbourg, contenaient en 1918 une population en grande majorité hongroise. Il est évident que la Hongrie ne pourrait, même dans l'esprit des accords de Munich, renoncer a ces villes. Neanmoins, faisant preuve une fois de plus d'un large esprit de conciliation, le Gouvernement Royal de Hongrie propose des plébiscites pour les territoires en question situés entre la ligne proposée par le Gouvernement Royal de Hongrie et celle marquée dans le projet que Votre Excellence a bien voulu me remettre par le note susindiquée. Les plébiscites devraient avoir lieu au plus tard jusqu'au 30 novembre 1938 à base du principe que seules les personnes ayant habité le 28 octobre 1918 dans ces territoires ou y nées avant cette date, ainsi que leurs descendants, auraient le droit de vote. Le plébiscite devrait être effectué séparément en huit sections, indiquées dans la carte ci-jointe. Les troupes tchécoslovaques devraient évacuer ces territoires jusqu'au 1er novembre courant et leur administration devrait être remise jusqu'au 15 novembre courant à des organes internationaux. (Carte)

Quant à Presbourg où aucune nationalité n'avait le majorité absolue en 1918, le Gouvernement Hongrois propose des conversations spéciales faisant suite aux négociations présentes.

Etant donné qu'il y a certaines petites divergences d'importance uniquement locale, qui ne sont pas comprises dans les territoires réservés aux plébiscites, des conversations directes entre les deux Gouvernements devraient être envisagées à cet effet. •

3. La Hongrie est animée du désir de jeter les fondements d'une situation stable, susceptible de rendre possible la cohabitation pacifique de toutes les nations établies dans cette partie de l'Europe centrale. Ce but ne saurait être atteint, de notre avis, qu'en accordant à toutes les nationalités, et naturellement aussi aux Ruthènes, la possibilité de disposer d'eux mêmes sous la forme d'un plébiscite en presence d'un controle international. Les nouvelles frontières de la Tchécoslovaquie ne pourraient être garanties par le Hongrie que sous cette condition.

4. Dans le cas où le Gouvernement Tchécoslovaque se verrait dans l'impossibilité d'accepter les plébiscites prévus plus haut, le Gouvernement Royal de Hongrie, de sa part, serait disposé de soumettre tout le territoire en litige y compris Presbourg—ainsi que nos demandes mentionnées sous No. 3 à un arbitrage. Cet arbitrage serait exercé pour les régions de l'ouest, c'est-à-dire de Presbourg jusqu'á la section 5 (voir la carte annexée) par l'Italie et l'Allemagne, pour les régions de l'est, c'est-à-dire les sections 6 à 8, par l'Italie, l'Allemagne et la Pologne. Les deux parties s'engageraient d'ores et déjà de se soumettre à la sentence arbitrale.

Vu la tension dangereuse de la situation actuelle, le Gouvernement Royal de Hongrie s'est hâté de répondre en 48 heures à la proposition de Votre Excellence et pour les mêmes raisons le Gouvernement Royal espère sérieusement que le Gouvernement de la République voudra bien faire du même empressement en la matire.

Veuillez agréer, Monsieur le Ministre, etc . . .

Wettstein

51.

Note tchécoslovaque, 26 octobre 1938[1]

No. 151.232/II/1-38　　　　　　　　　Praha, le 26 octobre 1938

Monsieur le Ministre,

Le Gouvernement tchécoslovaque a soumis à un examen attentif et approfondi les propositions du Gouvernement hongrois que Votre Excellence a bien voulu me transmettre par sa lettre 39/b du 24 octobre 1938.

Le Gouvernement tchécoslovaque se permet de faire ressortir une fois de plus que les négociations actuelles ne peuvent avoir trait qu'à la question de la minorité hongroise. En effet, les points 1 et 2 du Protocole additionnel de l'Accord du Munich du 29 septembre 1938 ne parlant que des minorités polonaise et hongroise, d'autres problèmes ethniques doivent rester en dehors du cadre des négociations actuelles.

En ce qui concerne la question de la minorité hongroise, le Gouvernement tchécoslovaque reste animé du désir sincere d'arriver à une solution franche, rapide et complète. C'est dans ce but qu'il a présenté le 22 octobre des propositions qui concernent tout le territoire national uni hongrois (geschlossener Volksboden). Ces propositions ont été transmises comme base générale aux négociations nouvelles auxquelles resteraient réservées des modifications ultérieures.

---

[1]*La Documentation*, p. 30.

Le Gouvernement hongrois ne considérant pas ces propositions comme satisfaisantes, le Gouvernement tchécoslovaque est d'accord pour soumettre la question de la minorité hongroise à une décision arbitrale de l'Allemagne et de l'Italie, signataires de l'accord de Munich. L'adjonction éventuelle d'autres arbitres devrait être laissée à la décision de ces deux Puissances elles-mêmes. Si ces deux Puissances donnaient suite à la proposition hongroise concernant la Pologne, le Gouvernement tchécoslovaque propose que la Roumanie y soit également associée.

Le décision arbitrale devrait fixer les modalités et les délais de l'évacuation par les troupes et les autorités hongroises. Le Gouvernement tchécoslovaque propose qu'une commission d'experts militaires hongrois et tchécoslovaques se réunisse de suite pour préparer et accélérer l'execution des mesures nécessaires.

Veuillez agréer, Monsieur le ministre, etc . . .

Chvalkovský

52.
Note hongroise, 27 octobre 1938[1]

529/I - 1938   Prague, le 27 octobre 1938

Monsieur le Ministre,

En réponse à la Note de Votre Excellence no. 151.323/II-1/38, en date du 26 octobre courant, j'ai l'honneur de vous communiquer ce qui suit:

Le Gouvernement Royal de Hongrie regrette que le Gouvernement de la République Tchécoslovaque passe entièrement sous silence la question des plébiscites proposés par le Gouvernement Hongrois. Cette attitude du Gouvernement de la République Tchécoslovaque a surpris le Gouvernement Royal Hongrois d'autant plus que sa proposition correspondait entièrement à l'esprit de l'accord de Munich, dont le Gouvernement de la République Tchécoslovaque s'est inspiré jusqu'ici dans toutes ses négociations. Le Gouvernement de la Republiqué prétend dans sa Note précitée "que les négociations actuelles ne peuvent avoir trait qu'à la question de la minorité hongroise" puisque "les points 1 et 2 du Protocole additionel de l'Accord de Munich du 29 septembre 1938 ne parlent que des minorités polonaise et hongroise." S'il est vrai que ces accords ne mentionnent textuellement que les Allemands, les Polonais et les Hongrois, néanmoins il n'est pas contestable que lesdits accords

---

[1]*La Documentation*, p. 30.

posent comme base de la nouvelle reconstruction de la République Tchécoslovaque l'autodétermination des peuples. Par consequent, le droit de disposer d'eux-mêmes par voie de plébiscite ne peut être réfusé aux minorités qui le réclament. Tout en déplorant le point de vue contraire du Gouvernement de la République, le Gouvernement Royal se voit contraint de maintenir son attitude.

Dans sa note précitée, le Gouvernement tchécoslovaque se déclare d'être disposé d'accepter l'arbitrage de l'Allemagne et de l'Italie, ce qui, de l'avis du Gouvernement Royal implique l'obligation de se soumettre d'avance à la décision desdites Puissances. Il est entendu que la compétence des arbitres ne s'etend qu'aux territoires en litige et non à ceux sur lesquels un accord existe déjà entre les deux Gouvernements et l'occupation desquels par des troupes hongroises a été déjà proposée dans ma Note de 24 courant.

La composition et la mise en oeuvre de l'arbitrage devraient être remises, de l'avis du Gouvernement Royal, aux Grandes Puissances intéressées.

En ce qui concerne la proposition que "la décision arbitrale devrait fixer les modalités et les délais de l'evacuation par les troupes et les autorités tchécoslovaques des territoires à céder et de son occupation par les troupes et les autorités hongroises", le Gouvernement Royal est de l'avis que cette proposition ne peut se rapporter qu'aux territoires en litige. C'est pour cette raison que le Gouvernement accepte volontiers l'offre de pourparlers directes et immédiats entre les experts militaires hongrois et tchécoslovaques, en vue de préparer et d'accélérer l'exécution des mesures nécessaires. A cet effet, l'attaché militaire à Prague se mettra en contact direct avec les autorités militaires compétentes tchécoslovaques.

Le Gouvernement Royal de Hongrie prend connaissance avec satisfaction de ce que le Gouvernement Tchécoslovaque reste animé du désir sincère d'arriver à une solution franche, rapide et complète.

Le Gouvernement Hongrois rappelle au souvenir du Gouvernement de la République Tchécoslovaque que dès le commencement des négociations il a toujours attribué la plus grande importance à une solution aussi rapide que possible de la question territoriale entre les deux Etats et qu'il déclinait toute responsabilité pour les conséquences qui pourraient résulter de la prolongation des pourparlers.

Veuillez agréer, Monsieur le Ministre, etc . . .

Wettstein

146

53.

Note tchécoslovaque, 28 octobre 1938[1]

No. 152.470/II-1/1938   Praha, le 28 octobre 1938

Monsieur le Ministre,

En réponse à la note de Votre Excellence no. 529/I-1938 du 27 octobre, mon Gouvernement me charge de vous communiquer ce que suit:

Le Gouvernement tchécoslovaque constate avec satisfaction que le Gouvernement hongrois est d'accord pour recourir à l'arbitrage de l'Allemagne et de l'Italie avec l'obligation de se soumettre d'avance à la décision desdites Puissances.

Il maintient son point de vue exposé dans les notes précedentes et fait ressortir entre autres de nouveau que les négociations actuelles ne peuvent avoir trait qu'à la question de la minorité hongroise. Il est très heureux d'être en parfait accord avec le Gouvernement hongrois pour "attribuer la plus haute importance à une solution aussi rapide que possible de la question territoriale entre les deux Etats." Il a en outre une pleine confiance dans l'arbitrage et il est sûr qu'il en est de même pour le Gouvernement hongrois qui a suggéré cette procédure.

C'est pour ces raisons qu'il a l'honneur de faire les propositions suivantes:

1. Dans les 24 heures après la réception de la présente note par le Gouvernement du Budapest, les deux Gouvernements prieront l'Allemagne et l'Italie d'arbitrer leurs différends.

2. Si le Gouvernement hongrois croit devoir maintenir son point de vue, d'après lequel un accord existerait déjà concernant certains territoires, point de vue auquel le Gouvernement tchécoslovaque ne peut s'associer, mon Gouvernement propose dans l'intérêt d'une solution rapide que les arbitres se prononcent eux-mêmes aussi sur cette différence de vues.

3. En ce qui concerne la question de l'occupation à laquelle se réfère la note du 27 octobre, le Gouvernement tchécoslovaque est sûr que la décision arbitrale la réglera le plus rapidement possible. Les milieux militaires compétents tchécoslovaques se sont d'ailleurs déjà mis en rapport avec l'attaché militaire hongrois à Prague pour procéder à des échanges de vue dans ce but.

Le Gouvernement tchécoslovaque espère fermement que le Gouvernement hongrois trouvera possible de s'associer sans retard à ces propositions. Ce serait la voie la plus rapide pour arriver au but souhaité par les deux Gouvernements.

Veuillez agréer, Monsieur le Ministre, etc. . .

Chvalkovský

---

[1]*La Documentation*, p. 31.

147

54.

Note hongroise, 29 octobre 1938[1]

549/I-1938   Prague, le 29 octobre 1938

Monsieur le Ministre,

En réponse à la Note No. 152.470/II-1/1938, en date du 28
octobre courant, j'ai d'ordre de mon Gouvernement, l'honneur de porter
à la connaissance de Votre Excellence que le Gouvernement Royal de
Hongrie s'est déjà adressé aux Grandes Puissances intéressées avec la
prière de se charger de l'arbitrage. Il saurait gré au Gouvernement de la
République Tschécoslovaque s'il voulait bien le faire également dans les
24 heures qu'il propose.

Le Gouvernement Royal de Hongrie réserve son attitude ultérieure
jusqu'à l'arrivée de la réponse des Grandes Puissances concernant l'acceptation de l'arbitrage.

Veuillez agréer, Monsieur le Ministre, etc. . .

Wettstein

―――――――――

[1]*La Documentation*, p. 31.

55.

Note tchécoslovaque, 29 octobre 1938[1]

153.093/II-1/1938   Praha, le 29 octobre 1938

En réponse à votre lettre No. 549/I-1938 en date d'aujour-d'hui,
j'ai l'honneur de porter à votre connaissance que le Gouvernement
Tchécoslovaque s'est de son côté empressé de demander à l'Allemagne
et à l'Italie de se charger de l'arbitrage.

Le Gouvernement Tchécoslovaque réserve également son attitude
ultérieure jusqu'à l'arrivée de la réponse des puissances ci-mentionnées
concernant l'acceptation de l'arbitrage.

Veuillez agréer, Monsieur le Ministre, etc. . .

Chvalkovský

―――――――――

[1]*La Documentation*, p. 31. On the 29th of October each of the two governments addressed a note to Germany and to Italy, asking them to arbitrate the dispute. The two
Powers having accepted in principle the function of arbitrators, and the Hungarian and
Czechoslovak governments having declared, on October 31st, to be ready to accept without reservation and as definitive an arbitral decision, and to execute it immediately, the
governments of Germany and Italy agreed to pronounce an arbitral sentence. To this
effect the foreign ministers of Germany and Italy decided to meet in Vienna on November
2, 1938. (Editor's note in *La Documentation Internationale*.)

56.

Note tchécoslovaque, 31 octobre 1938[1]

638.-1938   Budapest, 1938, október 31

A la suite de l'échange des notes verbales Nos. 610 et 624/38 émanant de la Légation de la République Tchécoslovaque et de la note du Ministère Royal des Affaires Etrangères No. 3599/pol. cette Légation se croit en dèvoir de fournir en complément à son aid-mémoire joint à la note verbale No. 610/38 un supplément d'informations étayant le bienfondé des faits y exposés.

Tout aussi attachée que le Gouvernement Hongrois aux méthodes pacifiques et munie d'une patience tout aussi exemplaire la Légation de la République Tchécoslovaque, afin de donner une preuve tangible de la justesse de ses assertions se voit forcée de joindre à la présente note les copies d'une série de documents tendant à prouver que les regrettables incidents qui se produisent en Russie Subcarpathique, ne sont pas la conséquence de l'ébranlement de l'authorité tant administrative que militaire, mais bien d'une tentative de coup de main conçu en dehors des frontières de ce pays, et exécuté par les éléments appartenant à l'armée régulière hongroise, conviction étayée par copie des documents ci-joints, documents que le Ministère Royal des Affaires Etrangères voudra étudier dans le même esprit de justice qui nous anime.

C'est pourqoi la Légation Tchécoslovaque estime que malgré la bonne foi de la note du Ministère Royal No. 3599/pol. la teneur n'en est pas exacte et que les incidents exposés par les notes emanant de la Légation Tchécoslovaque ne sauraient être qualifiés de suspicion, puisque les faits y cités se trouvent corroborés par la réalité et prouvés par les documents ci-joints.

(unsigned copy)

[1]*Diplomáciai iratok*, II, 881.

57.

Note tchécoslovaque, 31 octobre 1938[1]

639.-1938   Budapest, 1938, október 31

Faisant suite à la conversation que le Conseiller de cette Légation, Dr. P. Fisa a eue avec le Conseiller de Légation, M. de Kuhl, au Ministère des Affaires Etrangères le 26 October, la Légation Tchécoslovaque se voit obligée de saisir le Gouvernement Hongrois d'un incident qui s'ajoute à la série de transgressions et violations de la frontière tchécoslovaque si fréquentes ces derniers temps.

[1]*Diplomáciai iratok*, II, 881-82.

Il s'agit en l'occurence des faits suivants: Un avion tchécoslovaque d'observation survolait le 24 crt vers 15 heures le territoire tchécoslovaque aux environs de Komárno à une distance d'au moins 10 km en arrière de la frontière. Deux unités de l'armée de l'air hongroise franchissant le Danube et la frontière tchécoslovaque à une courte distance à l'oueste de ladite ville, foncèrent sur ledit avion d'observation qui eut à subir le feu d'un des aviateurs hongrois, attaque qui eut pour résultat d'obliger l'observateur tchécoslovaque blessé d'atterrir avec son avion en feu; la cause qui a déterminé cette brusque attaque paraît absolument inexplicable, car la mission d'observation de l'aviateur tchécoslovaque n'avait manifestement aucun caractère de provocation, puisqu'il se trouvait à l'interieur du territoire tchécoslovaque; les intentions pacifiques démontre d'ailleurs déjà le fait qu'il n'avait à bord aucune munition lui permettant de répondre au feu de l'avion agresseur.

En portant ce qui précède à la connaissance du Ministère Royal la Légation Tchécoslovaque se permet de Le prier de vouloir bien soumettre cet incident aux autorités compétents en vue d'une enquête et espère que le Ministère Royal des Affaires Etrangères voudra bien lui en communiquer les résultats en temps utile.

(unsigned copy)

58.

Lettre de ministre Kánya à Galeazzo Ciano[1]

Vienne, le 2 novembre 1938

Arrivant à la frontière hongroise, je m'empresse d'exprimer réitérément à Votre Excellence toutes mes reconnaissances pour les bons soins par lesquels vous vous êtes chargé, en plein accord avec le Gouvernement du Reich, de la solution de la question territoriale hungaro-tchécoslovaque. Je suis convaincu que la décision arbitrale prompte et rapide que vient de prendre la Haute Instance contribuera largement à l'apaisement des esprits et à la pacification de cette partie de l'Europe Centrale. La décision arbitrale de Vienne témoigne une fois de plus que l'Axe Rome-Berlin est une base solide de la paix mondiale.

Veuillez agréer, Monsieur le Ministre, l'expression de mes sentiments amicalement dévoués.

Kánya

---

[1]*Diplomáciai iratok*, II, 885. A similar telegram was sent by Kánya to Herr von Ribbentrop. Prime Minister Imrédy sent telegrams of appreciation to Mussolini and Hitler, respectively.

MAPS

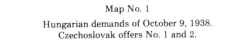

Map No. 1

Hungarian demands of October 9, 1938.
Czechoslovak offers No. 1 and 2.

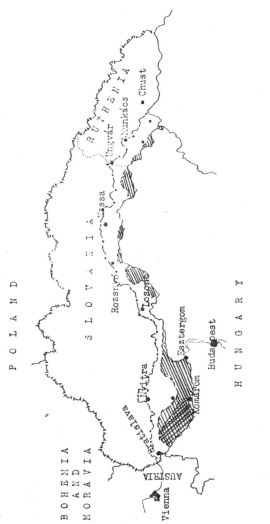

Symbols:

I I I I I ... Northern border of Hungary before 1919

——————— ... Borders created in 1919.

— · — · — ... Borderline claimed by Hungary on October 9, 1938

[hatched] ... First Czechoslovak offer (Csallóköz)

[hatched] ... Second Czechoslovak offer

· · · · · · · · ... Borderline between Slovakia and Ruthenia

Map No. 2
Third Czechoslovak offer and the eight contested zones

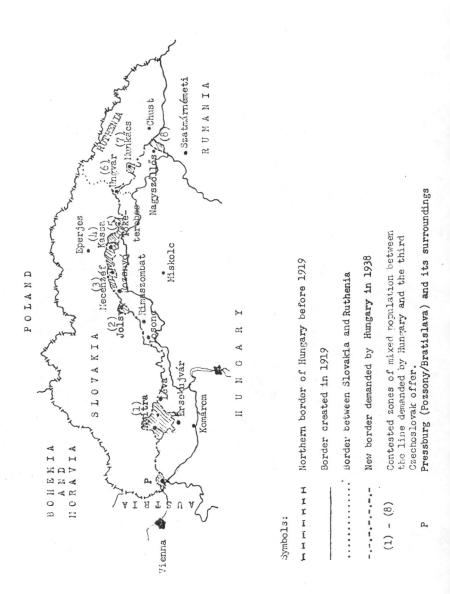

Symbols:

Ⅰ Ⅰ Ⅰ Ⅰ Ⅰ   Northern border of Hungary before 1919

·········· Border created in 1919

——————— Border between Slovakia and Ruthenia

-·-·-·-·-·-·- New border demanded by Hungary in 1938

(1) - (8)   Contested zones of mixed population between
            the line demanded by Hungary and the third
            Czechoslovak offer.

P   Pressburg (Pozsony/Bratislava) and its surroundings

Map No. 3
Changes effected by the Vienna Award

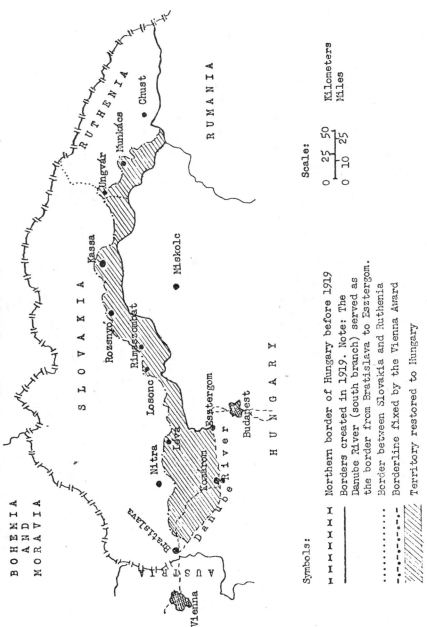

Scale:

Kilometers
Miles

```
0    25  50
0    10  25
```

Symbols:

I I I I I I I   Northern border of Hungary before 1919
                 Borders created in 1919. Note: The
─────────   Danube River (south branch) served as
                 the border from Bratislava to Esztergom.
. . . .   Border between Slovakia and Ruthenia
.-.-.-.-.-.   Borderline fixed by the Vienna Award
/////////   Territory restored to Hungary

POLAND

BOHEMIA
AND
MORAVIA

AUSTRIA

Vienna

Bratislava

Danube River

SLOVAKIA

Nitra

Ipra

Komárom

Losonc

Rimaszombat

Rozsnyó

Kassa

Miskolc

Esztergom

Budapest

HUNGARY

Ungvár

Munkács

RUTHENIA

Chust

RUMANIA

BIBLIOGRAPHY

Books

Ádám, Magda. *Magyarország és a Kisantant a harmincas években.* Budapest: Akadémiai Kiadó, 1968.

Beck, Jozef. *Final Report.* New York: Robert Speller & Sons, 1957.

Benes, Eduard. *Memoirs. From Munich to New War and Victory.* Boston: Houghton Mifflin, 1954.

Bromke, Adam, and Rakowska-Harmstone, Teresa (eds.). *The Communist States in Disarray, 1965-1971.* Minneapolis: University of Minnesota Press, 1972.

Brzezinski, Zbigniew K. *The Soviet Bloc: Unity and Conflict.* Rev. & Enl. Ed. Cambridge, Mass.: Harvard University Press (1960, 1967).

Carr, Edward Hallett. *The Twenty Years' Crisis, 1919-1939.* 2d. ed. London: Macmillan, 1949.

Celovsky, Boris. *Das Münchener Abkommen 1938.* Stuttgart: Deutsche Verlags-Anstalt, 1958.

Ciano, Galeazzo. *Hidden Diary 1937-1938.* Transl. by Andreas Mayor. New York: E.P. Dutton and Co., 1953.

Claude, Inis L., Jr. *National Minorities: An International Problem.* Cambridge, Mass.: Harvard University Press, 1955.

Cobban, Alfred. *National Self-Determination.* Chicago: University of Chicago Press, 1947.

Corbett, Percy E. *Law and Society in the Relations of States.* New York: Harcourt, Brace and Co., 1951.

Deak, Francis. *Hungary at the Paris Peace conference.* New York: Columbia University Press, 1942.

Eisler, Pavel. *Munich; A Retrospect.* Prague: Orbis, 1958.

Fenwick, Charles G. *International Law.* 3d ed. New York: Appleton, 1954.

Hill, Norman. *Claims to Territory in International Law and Relations.* London: Oxford University Press, 1945.

Hoensch, Jörg Konrad. *Der ungarische Revisionismus und die Zerschlagung der Tschechoslovakei.* Tübingen: Mohr (Siebeck), 1967.

House, Edward M., and Seymour, Charles (eds.). *What Really Happened at Paris: The Story of the Peace Conference, 1918-1919.* New York: Charles Scribner's Sons, 1921.

Hutton, D.G. *Survey after Munich.* Boston: Little, Brown & Co., 1939.

Juhász, Gyula. *Magyarország külpolitikája, 1919-1945.* Budapest: Kossuth Könyvkiadó, 1969.

Karsai Elek. *A budai Sándor-palotában történt, 1919-1941.* 3d ed. Budapest, Táncsics Könyvkiadó, 1967.

Karsai, Elek. *"Országgyarapitás"—Országvesztés.* Part I, 1933-1939. Budapest: Kossuth Könyvkiadó, 1961.

Kertesz, Stephen D. *Diplomacy in a Whirlpool: Hungary between Nazi Germany and Soviet Russia.* South Bend: University of Notre Dame Press, 1953.

Kis, Aladár. *Magyarország külpolitikája a második világháboru előestéjén (1938 november - 1939 szeptember).* Budapest: Kossuth Könyvkiadó, 1963.

Kordt, Erich. *Nicht aus den Akten . . .* Stuttgart: Union Deutsche Verlagsgesellschafft, 1950.

Král, Václav. *O Masarykově a Benešově kontrarevolučni protisovětské politice.* Praha: Státni nakl. politické literatury, 1953.

Laffan, R.D.G., et. al. *Survey of International Affairs 1938* (Royal Institute of International Affairs). Vols. I, II, and III. London: Oxford University Press, 1951, 1953.

Lettrich, Jozef. *History of Modern Slovakia.* New York: Frederick A. Praeger, 1955.

Macartney, Carlyle A. *A History of Hungary 1929-1945.* Vol. I. New York: Frederick A. Praeger, 1957.

Mikus, Joseph A. *Slovakia. A Political History: 1918-1950.* Milwaukee: The Marquette University Press, 1963.

Namier, Lewis B. *Diplomatic Prelude, 1938-1939.* London: Macmillan, 1948.

Orcival, Francois d'. *Le Danube etait noir; la cause de la Slovaquie independante.* Paris: la Table ronde, 1968.

156

Ránki, György. *Emlékiratok és valóság Magyarország második világháborús szerepéről*. Budapest: Kossuth Könyvkiadó, 1964.

Révay, István. *Die im Belvedere gezogene ungarisch-slowakische Grenze*. Budapest: Athenaeum nyomda, 1941.

' Ripka, Hubert. *Munich: Before and After. A Fully Documented Czechoslovak Account of the Crises of September 1938 and March 1939*. Translated from the manuscript by Ida Sindelkova and Comdr. Edgar P. Young. London: Victor Gollancz Ltd., 1939.

Ross, Alf. *A Textbook of International Law*. London: Longmans, Green and Co., 1947.

Seton-Watson, Hugh. *Eastern Europe between the Wars, 1918-1941*. Cambridge: The University Press, 1945.

Seton-Watson, R.W. *From Munich to Danzig*. 3d ed. rev. London: Methuen and Co., 1939.

Sirchich, László. *Belvedere-től Kassáig. A felvidéki magyarság útja az első bécsi döntéstől a "Košicky" Programig*. Cleveland, Ohio: By the Author, 1969.

Stone, Julius. *Legal Controls of International Conflicts*. New York: Rinehart & Co., 1954.

Taborsky, Eduard. *The Czechoslovak Cause: An Account of the Problems of International Law in Relation to Czechoslovakia*. London: Witherby, 1944.

Thomson, S. Harrison. *Czechoslovakia in European History*. Rev. ed. Princeton: Princeton University Press, 1953.

Tilkovszky, Loránt. *Revizió és nemzetiségpolitika Magyarországon (1938-1941)*. Budapest: Akadémiai Kiadó, 1967.

Ullein-Reviczky, Antal. *Guerre Allemande, Paix Russe: Le Drame Hongrois*. Neuchatel: Editions de la Baconniere, 1947.

Várva, Ferdinand. *Viedenská arbitráž dôsledok Mníchova*. Bratislava: Osveta, 1963.

Visscher, Charles de. *Theory and Reality in Public International Law*. Translated by P.E. Corbett. Princeton: Princeton University Press, 1957.

Werth, Alexander. *France and Munich Before and After the Surrender*. New York: Harper, 1939.

Wheeler-Bennett, John W. *Munich: Prologue to Tragedy.* New York: Duell, Sloan and Pearce, 1948.

Wiskemann, Elizabeth. *Prologue to War.* London: Oxford University Press, 1940.

Public Documents

Ádám, Magda, ed. *A müncheni egyezmény létrejötte és Magyarország külpolitikája, 1936-1938.* Vol. II of *Diplomáciai iratok Magyarország külpolitikájához, 1936-1945.* Ed. by Magyar Tudományos Akadémia Történettudományi Intézete. 4 vols. Budapest: Akadémiai Kiadó, 1962-70.

Balasko, André, ed. "II. Frontières Tchécoslovaques 1938." *La Documentation Internationale Politique, Juridique, et Economique.* 6me Année, Mars-Avril 1939.

Craster, H.H.E., ed. *Speeches on Foreign Policy by Viscount Halifax.* London: Oxford University Press, 1940.

Curtis, Monica, ed. *Documents on International Affairs 1938.* (Royal Institute of International Affairs.) Vols. II and III. London: Oxford University Press, 1943.

Documents Secrets du Ministère des Affaires Étrangères d'Allemagne. Traduit du Russe par Madeleine et Michael Eristov. Vol. II (Hongrie). Paris: Éditions Paul Dupont, 1946.

France, Assemblée Nationale. *Les Événements Survenus en France de 1933 a 1945. Temoignages et Documents Recueillis par la Commission d'Enquête Parlamentaire.* Paris: Presses Universitaires de France, n.d.

France, Ministère des Affaires Étrangères. *The French Yellow Book. Diplomatic Documents 1938-1939.* London: Hutchinson and Co. Ltd., 1940.

Great Britain, Parliament. *Parliamentary Debates. House of Commons.* Fifth Series. Vols. 341, 342, 345. London: His Majesty's Stationery Office, 1938-1939.

Horthy, Miklós, nagybányai. *The Confidential Papers of Admiral Horthy.* (Miklós Szinay and László Szücs, compilers.) Budapest: Corvina Press, 1965.

Hudson, Manley O., ed. *International Legislation. A Collection of the Texts of Multipartite International Instruments of General Interest.* Vol. VIII (1938-1941). Washington: Carnegie Endowment for International Peace, 1949.

The Hungarian Question in the British Parliament. Speeches in the House of Lords and the House of Commons from 1919 to 1930. London: Grant Richards, 1933.

Hungary, Ministry for Foreign Affairs. *Hungary and the Conference of Paris.* Vol. IV. Budapest: Hungarian Ministry for Foreign Affairs, 1947.

International Military Tribunal. *Trial of the Major War Criminals Before the International Military Tribunal.* Vol. XXXV. Nuremberg: International Military Tribunal, 1949.

Jedrzejewicz, Waclaw, ed. *Diplomat in Berlin 1933-1939. Papers and Memoirs of Józef Lipski, Ambassador of Poland.* New York: Columbia University Press, 1968.

Klochko, Valentin F., ed. *New Documents on the History of Munich.* Prague: Orbis, 1958.

Kràl, Václav, ed. *Das Abkommen von München 1938; tschechoslovakische diplomatische Dokumente 1937-1939.* Prague: Academia, 1968.

Magyar Tudományos Akadémia Történettudományi Intézete. *Magyarország és a második világháború. Titkos diplomáciai okmányok a háború előzményeihez és történetéhez.* 3d ed. (Magda Ádám, Gyula Juhász and Lajos Kerekes, compilers.) Budapest: Kossuth Könyvkiadó, 1966.

Sudetendeutscher Rat. *München 1938. Dokumente sprechen.* 3d enl. ed. Munich: Wolf, 1965.

U.S. Department of State. *Documents on German Foreign Policy 1918-1945. From the Archives of the German Foreign Ministry.* Series D (1937-1945), Vols. II and IV. Washington: U.S. Government Printing Office, 1949-1956.

U.S. Department of State. *Foreign Relations of the United States: Diplomatic Papers, 1938.* Vol. I. Washington: U.S. Government Printing Office, 1955.

Woodward, E.L., and Butler, Rohan, eds. *Documents on British Foreign Policy 1919-1939.* 3d Series, Vols. II and III (1938-1939). London: His Majesty's Stationery Office, 1950.

Articles

Bowman, Isaiah. "The Strategy of Territorial decision." *Foreign Affairs,* XXIV (January, 1946). 176-194.

Campbell, John C. "The European Territorial Settlement." *Foreign Affairs,* XXVI (October, 1947). 196-218.

"Idézetek, Vélemények és Nyilatkozatok." *Bulletin of the Research Institute for Minority Studies on Hungarians Attached to Czechoslovakia and Carpatho-Ruthenia* (New York), II (July-September, 1957), 22-29.

Ránki, György. "Adatok a magyar külpolitikához a Csehszlovákia elleni agresszió idején (1937-1939)." Part I. *Századok,* LXXXXIII, No. 1 (1959), 117-158. Part II. *Századok,* LXXXXIII, No. 2-4 (1959), 356-372.

Rogers, Lindsay. "Munich: American Opinion and Policy." *The Political Quarterly* (London), X (January-March, 1939).

Roucek, Joseph S. "Europe After Munich." *Social Science,* XIV (January, 1939). 17-22.

Taborsky, Eduard. "'Munich', the Vienna Arbitration and International Law." *Czechoslovak Yearbook of International Law,* 1942, pp. 21-38.

Taborsky, Edward. "Benes and the Soviets." *Foreign Affairs,* XXVII (January, 1949). 302-314.

Varga, László, ed. "A Magyar Forradalom és Szabadságharc a Hazai Rádióadások Tükrében." *Magyarországi Események* (Free Europe Press), VIII (1956 Október 23 - November 9). 1-376.

Wagner, Francis S. "Political Historiography and Its Bibliography in Post-1945 Central and Eastern Europe." *Studies for a New Central Europe* (Mid-European Research Institute, New York), Series 3, No. 1 (1971-72). 73-92.

Wright, Quincy. "The Munich Settlement and International Law." *American Journal of International Law,* XXXIII (January, 1939). 12-32.

Index